Praise for *Own Your Freedom*

This book is dynamite. David and Dan demolish the outdated "traditional" approach to life, career, and wealth we've all been taught and they offer a robust alternative path to success.

Dustin S. Burleson, DDS, MBA

As an attorney running a successful practice, I have been following (and benefitting from) the work of David Phelps and Dan Kennedy for years. While much of their combined work to date has been in the area of "how do I build a successful practice?" this book breaks new ground because it answers the question that many of us have: how do we maximize the product of all that work we put into building a successful professional career? David and Dan look at wealth-building and wealth preservation differently than most people and this is why you should read this book, no matter where you are on your career/ wealth-building journey. It will provoke your thinking and may, at times, irritate you. This is good. I will be recommending this book to my highly successful attorney friends.

Ben Glass, founder, BenGlassLaw and Great Legal Marketing

Own Your Freedom is the blueprint for taking responsibility and owning your life. It includes all the information, mindset, and tools you need to succeed in our volatile economy while laying out the strategies to compete in this new era of radical change.

Daniel Marcos, CEO Growth Institute
www.GrowthInstitute.com

If you're accustomed to believing the press and what others tell us on a daily basis, then this book is not for you. If you challenge groupthink and want to set your own sail, enlarge your capacity, and create Freedom in your life, then grab this book and study it nonstop.

Lee Milteer, author and professional speaker
at www.Milteer.com

Buckle up! You are in for the ride of your financial life. What Dr. Phelps and Mr. Kennedy are providing here in this most powerful wealth-building book is a dynamic and very personal adventure that will lead you to a promised land of riches in far more forms than just money. In this book, Dr. Phelps and Dan prove that wealth is about so much more than dollars in your bank account—it is foundational for everything in your life because it is the foundation for your freedom.

Speaking from personal and intimate experience as an observer, client, follower, colleague, and close personal friend, I know there's not two others like them. What they say works. And their combined in-the-trenches-experience of actually following their own advice, practicing what they preach, and being examples of developing sustainable wealth has stood the test of time despite multiple disruptionsin our always volatile world.

More importantly, I've witnessed firsthand their life-changing impact on countless other business owners and professionals who have heeded their advice, embraced their principles, and followed their strategies to a better life and business to achieve true financial independence, wealth in all forms, and ultimate liberation. Now you've got an opportunity to do the same. Your prosperity awaits, right here in your hands, with Dr. Phelps and Dan as your guides. And I assure you there is no more important journey you could be on than this one right here, because if you don't *Own Your Freedom*, you don't actually own your life or anything else in it.

Scott J. Manning, MBA, leading authority on the business of dentistry, author, and founder, www.DentalSuccessToday. com and www.MillionDollarMethods.com

David Phelps and Dan Kennedy have created the blueprint for achieving success, wealth, and freedom. More importantly, they have outlined the framework for mastering significance and joy through financial accomplishment. This is a timeless read for all of us.

Christopher Ryan, CEO, GoBundance

By now, even the most distracted citizen cannot help but notice the obvious shifts we are living through as a society. Economic, medical, political, and financial turmoil stains the pages of every news report. In a time where the only choice appears to be to pick a side, David and Dan make the case for a third path: one toward individual sovereignty. Their call, for those few of us willing to listen, is to own our freedom by building a path to get there. David and Dan have done this themselves. They are the product of the product. What they have done here is more than a clarion call, it is a road map to a future of your design. This book is not for everyone. Most will yield their freedom to the hoped-for benevolence of the authorities. For the rest of us, the call is clear—and now, finally, the map to its achievement is too.

Alastair J. Macdonald, founder, The Full Cycle Entrepreneur

To say that this book, *Own Your Freedom*, could not have been written at a more important time is maybe the understatement of all time. You may have a gut feeling that things are unsettled, and major change is happening all around you. You might even say things appear to be spinning out of control. Whether you bury your head in cable news, or you bury your head in the sand, hoping for things to get better or return to normal, understand this: major events are happening right now, all around us, that will have a huge impact in all of our lives.

There is a sea change going in this country and in the world, and while I am the furthest thing from an alarmist, I am educating myself as it relates to my financial health, which is tied directly to my freedom. *Own Your Freedom* is a very important book.

If you, like me, sometimes wonder where to turn for the straightforward, unvarnished truth, this book is a great start. I personally hold both David Phelps and Dan Kennedy in the highest regard, and their mission with this book is to wake you up, wake us all up, and show that we all have a role to play in protecting our freedoms. Reading this book, and passing it along to someone you care about, is a great first step in arming yourself.

Jim Palmer, The Dream Business Coach, www.GetJimPalmer.com

Freedom after 2020 has a new meaning to us all. It can no longer be taken for granted. You and your family's freedom depends on you taking bold actions now. This book will help you be prepared mentally to level up your financial literacy and actions, plus share with you proven strategies to help you truly *Own Your Freedom* and financial future.

Tom Beal, United States Marine Corps ('93-'97), founder of the www.MakeTodayGreat.com podcast.

In *Own Your Freedom: Sustainable Wealth for a Volatile World*, by David Phelps and Dan Kennedy, you get hard-hitting, proven, No BS advice from not just two very wealthy men, but more importantly two high-quality men. I've known both authors for over thirty years combined and have witnessed first-hand what they advocate, teach, and share within this book. Their teaching is spot-on and chock full of wisdom that has produced sustained results the past forty years during multiple ups and downs in the global economy. I could not put this book down and will be promoting it to my top clients and referral partners. Bravo gentleman on joining forces to share this timely and valuable wisdom with the world!

Tony Rubleski, bestselling author and business consultant, www.MindCaptureGroup.com

If David Phelps stands for one principle, it's creating freedom in your life. So many professionals follow the conventional advice that hard work will create security in your life. David flips that principle on its head. He shares his unique perspective on how to help other professionals take charge of their lives and secure their future. In *Own Your Freedom*, he offers concrete principles and steps to help you design your future, so you can take the real leap and get into action. By diversifying your skills, connecting with the right community, and using the benefits of investing in real estate, David lays out a plan to help his readers take their freedom into their own hands.

Dr. Laura Brenner, dentist, coach, and founder of Lolabees Career Coaching

Dr. David Phelps has done it again! If you follow the principles outlined in this book, David will help you take control over that which drives every entrepreneur: your Freedom. With the help of his mentor, Dan Kennedy, he will take you on a path of self-discovery and realization to define what your Freedom truly looks like. Define the steps you need to take, organize their priority, and create a solid plan for achieving them. Having practiced and lived what he discusses, I can't think of a better person to guide you down this path.

Dr. Christopher Phelps, DMD CMCT

I've spent twenty-plus years teaching my students that you are in business for *Freedom* and that everything should be set up to fit *you*! If you're ready to take control of your future and live life on your terms, then read, absorb, and follow the strategies in this brilliant book by my friend Dr. David Phelps! He is giving you a roadmap for creating the life you desire!

James Malinchak, star of ABC's hit TV show, Secret Millionaire, and the world's leading speaker trainer; founder of www.BigMoneySpeaker.com

David and Dan understand Freedom is waning and it's time to gather the reins and take control of our lives. Like guides through a dense forest, they take you from where you're at to financial security and peace of mind.

John Meis, DDS, CEO, The Team Training Institute; CEO, Spark Dental Network

Dr. David Phelps is a money patriot. He truly understands and explains in *Own Your Freedom* what money is and how it works in your best interest and not someone else's. Dan Kennedy's input enhances the message of creating your personal sovereignty. This information is the "Don't Tread on Me" way of reaching financial freedom!

Dr. Mart McClellan, president of Macro Wealth Management, charter member of the ForbesSpeakers Group, and orthodontist

Despite the occasional mediocre baseball player becoming a winning manager, or the unsuccessful actor becoming a great teacher of acting, it's better to have people who "did it" to tell us how to "do it." When it comes to "owning your freedom," especially your financial freedom, there are few people on the planet who have "done it" to the extent that David Phelps and Dan Kennedy have done it. And thank goodness they have written this book as a blueprint for us to do it, too.

Own Your Freedom: Sustainable Wealth for a Volatile World is a manual for a lifetime of financial freedom and a guide to preserving wealth from two guys who have done it better than anyone. If you are looking for quick tips on investing or faster ways to becoming a millionaire, this book is not for you; however, if you want a way to get rich slowly, with intention and independent thinking—and keep and preserve all of those riches for eternity—Phelps and Kennedy have the perfect prescription. And always with an eye on that prize while controlling your own destiny—rather than dishing off the responsibility to others—who rarely (if ever) deserve your trust. It's doubtful that "others" know more than you do either—and they definitely won't know more than you once you read *Own Your Freedom.*

Brian Kurtz, Titans Marketing and author of
Overdeliver and The Advertising Solution

David and Dan demolish the stranglehold of groupthink by challenging readers to question traditional thinking. *Own Your Freedom* is your true roadmap to a challenging new world filled with falsehoods.

Dr. Nathan Ho, dentist, entrepreneur,
and co-founder of EnvisionStars

Fine-tune your mindset, build your network, and improve your skills for achieving more personal and financial freedom now and in your future with the secrets in *Own Your Freedom.* A must to read and then reread.

Steven J. Anderson, founder, Total Patient Service Institute,
Crown Council, and Smiles for Life Foundation

I have known Dr. David Phelps for many years. I have also read just about every Dan Kennedy book published. This collaboration couldn't be more perfect. The time is now to wake up from a societal prison camp that lures with debt and instant gratification. Critical thinking is necessary to break the chains that bind us from experiencing freedom by choosing a different path. Inside *Own Your Freedom* you'll find the keys needed to unlock the doors to get there.

Cory Boatright, CEO, REIProfits

It is my absolute honor to share some thoughts on *Own Your Freedom* by Dr. David Phelps and the Professor of Harsh Reality, Dan Kennedy. The book demystifies and clarifies "money goals" – such as restructuring debt, creating passive income, leveraging sustainable assets – to ultimately create economic freedom where you can live the way you want and deserve. To be able to do so, we need to treat our financial goals the same way we treat our clinical and business goals, in a way that's educated, focused, adaptive, and intentional.

Dan Kennedy's writing in this book is genuinely provocative as always. His discussion on Group-Think and the "boring consistency" of success strategies will challenge how you think, who you associate with, and what to focus on despite the distractions of life, which are sometimes on a global scale.

I have known Dr. David Phelps for many years and have the privilege to observe his journey "from good to great." We are lucky because Dr. Phelps generously shares his knowledge in this book. I highly recommend taking notes while studying this book because it is the kind of book that challenges your thinking and helps you create your financial roadmap. Make sure you join Dr. Phelps in his next event, whether virtual or live, because the energy is always contagious, the knowledge is exceptional, and the success is beautifully celebrated.

Emily Letran, DDS, MS, CHPC, speaker, author, and certified high-performance coach

You are closer to freedom than you realize. My friend, David Phelps, will take you on an incredible journey that will guide you to new perspectives on what freedom is and how to live an extraordinary life.

Jim Ingersoll, real estate entrepreneur
and author of Cash Flow Now

Napoleon Hill's book *Think and Grow Rich* was a look at the fundamental characteristics of successful people. Dr. Phelps' *Own Your Freedom* is to freedom what Hill's book was to success. However, where Hill's book was a study in success, it lacked much of the 'how' required to achieve success. David's book is truly a roadmap for achieving freedom in one's life. There's no conjecture in this book. It's filled with firsthand experience from both Dr. Phelps and Dan Kennedy. Having known and worked with them very closely, I have witnessed both living everything they share in the pages of this book. Success is one thing. Freedom is another. You cannot have full success without freedom.

Ron Sheetz, Founder, RJ Media Magic

Hope is not a course of action! *Own Your Freedom* is a roadmap and guide for those looking to take control of their lives and create freedom. David and Dan smash traditional thinking and encourage you to focus on the business of your money!

Michael P. Abernathy, DDS, founder, Summit Practice Solutions

Author David Phelps is on a mission to lead you to *Own Your Freedom,* no matter the stage of your career. As thought leaders, Dr. David Phelps and Dan Kennedy challenge conventional paths to live life after one's active income ends. Divided into chapters focused on five key principles, the book will awaken your mind with a method that Dr. Phelps started teaching nearly ten years ago. Be ready to diversify your mind, think about a new skill set, and pivot away from the abundance goal to focus on cash-flow sustaining hard assets. There are many roads to freedom...you just need to find your own path.

Peter Farrehi, MD, Ann Arbor, Michigan

Own Your Freedom is the definitive summation and high-level overview of the principles and mindsets I have learned over the past four years within David Phelps's Freedom Founders Mastermind. It is David's written manifestation of the years of experience he has in both achieving his own freedom and helping professionals like me own our freedom as well. The additional insights from Dan Kennedy add an invaluable perspective that pairs with the mindset taught by Dr. Phelps. This book is a must-read, not just for those new to the idea of pursuing their own financial and personal freedom, but also for those of us already further along the freedom journey. The work of gaining financial independence and personal freedom of time, relationships, significance, and legacy is about 90 percent mindset and principles. *Own Your Freedom* is the most complete treatise on the topic I've yet to encounter. Congratulations, David and Dan, on creating a resource that will change lives and create ripples of legacy for generations to come!

Andy Baber, oral surgeon, Rogers, Arkansas

You are closer to financial freedom than you realize. The principles described in these pages are a clear "blueprint" for clarity. Sustainable cash flow is the key to achieving financial freedom, and it cannot be achieved by handing our savings over to others to manage. We need to be in the driver's seat—after all, no one cares for your money like you do. David and Dan outline a clear path that anyone can follow.

This book is not simply about growing your wealth. Though financial freedom may be the first step toward personal freedom, it is not the finish line. True freedom comes once we realize that money is not the primary driving force in our lives. Once we have the financial resources to focus on what really matters, the chains come off. Being free to pursue our purpose is where real freedom is found. David has been an integral part of our freedom journey, and I am so grateful for his friendship and insight!

Benjamin Jensen, DDS, and Sondra Jensen, South Dakota

This book provides excellent, to the point insight into Dr. Phelps's amazing, non-traditional approach to personal financial freedom. I've been a member of Freedom Founders for about a year and a half and have 100 percent changed my view toward personal finance. I'm totally out of the stock market and fully deployed in alternatives thanks to David's guidance. David's network is vast! I sleep soundly and love the monthly/quarterly cash flow. Dr. Phelps and Dan Kennedy's no-nonsense, straightforward approach is a sound blueprint for financial freedom.

Timothy R. Raborn, DDS, Baton Rouge, Louisiana

In my job, I often come across dentists who feel chained to their chairs. They're trading time for dollars, and have a murky financial future at best. Many want off the hamster wheel but have no idea how. This book answers that question. In it, the incomparable Dan Kennedy will fundamentally change how you view money and freedom. Dr. David Phelps will then bring it home with a playbook custom-made to help you break the handcuffs. Read this book, put its concepts to work, and start your journey to true freedom. You might just find it's closer than you think!

Bill Ladd, CPA, Duckett Ladd Dental CPAs and Advisors

This should be a must-read for everyone. Unfortunately, this book teaches non-traditional thinking and only those *searching* for it are lucky enough to find a book like this—especially if you have that small, nagging voice in your head saying, "Something is missing in life" or "I feel trapped." This book is an extraordinary collaboration on how to avoid the trap (if you're young enough), or on how to systematically remove yourself from the trap (if you're currently in it), and accelerate towards true Freedom. It gives you all the ingredients and the recipe for how to make the cake, but leaves it to you to take action and do the cooking.

Michael J. Dostal, DDS, Overland Park, Kansas

Another stellar and timely book from Dr. David Phelps with the added bonus of a collaboration with one of my favorite authors and thought leaders, Dan Kennedy. I was thrilled to learn from this latest book even more about investing. First, when investing we must start with our Principles, followed closely by our Strategy, and finally, implementing specific Tactics based on the first two. Unfortunately, many investors get the specific order incorrect and fail to reach their investment goals. The book also has an awesome and clear description of inflation and how it can hinder your investment outcomes. Thank you, David, for sharing your valuable time to write this book and educating so many. You are showing and teaching us another way!

Dr. James Rachor, investor, dentist, mentor,
and president of the Rachor Family Office

Own Your Freedom is such a powerful book. The concepts that David Phelps and Dan Kennedy explain are life-changing. The principles in this book are ideas that for thirty-five years of my dental carrier, I never understood or even had a clue they existed. I thought that working as a dentist at the chair was the only only way to freedom. Once David explained these to us and helped us understand there is another way, we were all in. To say that it was life-changing is an understatement.

Our life post-dentistry is beyond what we ever expected with the freedom to have two homes and travel as we please. The key to this book is understanding David's and Dan's principles, then taking action. It is a must-read if you want to have a different and better life. We now have time to mentor and give back. Thank you both for your insights and trail-blazing courage to not follow the herd.

Dr. Greg and Jackie Linney

This is *the book* that the dental profession has been waiting for and has needed for some time. It is an essential *must-read book*, not only for all graduating dentists but for *all dentists* to read not once, but many times over the course of their dental careers.

Nowhere in dental school is business explained to dentists in the way that Dr. David Phelps and Dan Kennedy have explained it in detail in *Own Your Freedom*. This is the textbook that had to be written. Dr. Omer Reed said that 95 percent of dentists reaching the age of 65 cannot afford to retire because they have failed to accumulate sufficient wealth to passively replace their dental income. And therein lies the tragedy. The gift of dental practice ownership has been squandered because of a lack of vital information.

But squander no more. Now, thanks to *Own Your Freedom*, dentists of all ages have the opportunity of turning their lives around and reaching their required number, so that they can now choose where they want to live, where they want to send their children to school, where they want to vacation to, and when and where they choose to retire to.

The best part about this book is that the authors have actually "*walked the walk.*" They have successfully practiced what they preach in this book. *Own Your Freedom* is not some make-believe philosophy gleaned by someone who just espoused some unproven theory. Rather, it is jam-packed full of tried, tested, and proven results.

If you want your dental practice to create for you the lifestyle that you deserve, then read and re-read this book. Ignore *Own Your Freedom* at your peril.

Dr. David Moffet, BDS, FPFA, CSP, former dental practice owner, author of the #1 Amazon Bestseller, *How To Build The Dental Practice Of Your Dreams: (Without Killing Yourself!) In Less Than 60 Days*

If you could own only one thing in your life, it should be your freedom. I've personally witnessed, with my own eyes, the creation of personal freedom for many people because of their connections to Dan Kennedy and Dr. David Phelps. I've watched them care for and impact lives through their education and actions. They not only taught people what to do, but made sure they did it!

This book contains real world experience, because Dan and Dr. Phelps have done it themselves – they own their freedom and you can too. How do I know it works? Besides watching them help others to freedom, they use the same principles I used twenty-six years ago to create my own personal freedom.

This book provides the principles for you to become free in all areas of your life. Once you get free, you can help others gain freedom, too. For decades I've studied what you can do to influence yourself and take control of your life, and this book provides the roadmap and the blueprint for you to *Own Your Freedom*. You will remember this day, when you started your freedom journey, as a key inflection point of your life. Take control, start your journey, and start reading it now!

Blaine Oelkers, America's Chief Results
Officer® and creator of Selfluence.com

OWN YOUR FREEDOM

OWN YOUR FREEDOM

Sustainable Wealth for a Volatile World

Dr. DAVID PHELPS, DDS with **DAN S. KENNEDY**

CONVERSATION PUBLISHING

Printed in the United States of America.

First paperback edition August 2021.

10 9 8 7 6 5 4 3 2 1

Front cover art by Monica Austin, Mocah Studio, LLC.
Full jacket and layout design by George Stevens, G Sharp Design, LLC.

ISBN 978-1-7359415-4-7 (print)
ISBN 978-1-7359415-5-4 (ebook)

Published by Conversation Publishing.
www.conversationpublishing.com

This book is dedicated to the logical, rational dreamer; the entrepreneur with vision and aspiration to follow his or her dreams; the small business owner, the capitalist, who through hard work and perseverance solves problems for others and adds to the economy at large; the self-reliant, who wants nothing from the government except the freedom to craft his or her own life.

ACKNOWLEDGMENTS

L ife is not a solo journey. I owe much gratitude to the many hundreds and thousands of people who have graced my life and been additive to my own abundance mindset and path to freedom. There is no doubt that I am a composite of many of the best characteristics of those with whom I have been blessed and have chosen to associate. I am a firm believer of Jim Rohn's often cited proclamation, "You are the average of the five people you spend the most time with."

The following is by no means a complete list – that would be impossible. As my co-author and mentor Dan Kennedy would say, "80 percent complete is good enough." And with that, thank you to the following who have sown into my life and helped me on my own path to Freedom:

Herschel R. Phelps, Sr.	Mike Crow	Jason Medley
Dr. Herschel R. Phelps, Jr.	David Frey	Cory Boatright
Marilyn Phelps	Carrie Wilkerson	Dr. Dustin Burleson
Kandace Phelps	Jonathan Sprinkles	Dr. John Meis
Jennifer Phelps	Michelle Prince	Dr. Emily Letran
Donna Phelps	Dr. Chandler George	Garrett Gunderson
Deborah Phelps Touslee	Matt Patterson	Norm Westervelt
Sarah Phelps Pyper	Jim Palmer	Roy Williams
James Malinchak	Tony Rubleski	Scott Manning

Adam Witty	John Groom. CPA	Dave Van Horn
Lee Milteer	Dr. John Mark Weaver	Dr. Bill Williams
Robin Robins	John Schaub	Dr. Ben Varner
Brian Kurtz	Peter Fortunato	Wendell Burgess
Mike Michalowicz	Jimmy Napier	Virginia Burgess
Amber Vilhauer	Glenn Stromberg	Joe Boshinski
Taki Moore	Ryan Parson	Lyle F. Wall
Dr. David Maloley	Mike Zlotnik	Dr. Pat Wahl
Jim Ingersoll	H. Quincy Long	Craig Simpson
Jim Sheils	Dyches Boddiford	Ron Phillips
Daniel Marcos	Bryan Binkholder	Patrick Precourt
Alastair MacDonald	Eddie Speed	Frank Rolfe
Shaun McCloskey	Ben Glass	Dr. Michelle
Chris Scappatura	Steven J. Anderson	Mudge-Riley
Burt Copeland	Dr. Howard Farran	Dr. Laura Brenner
Jack Miller	Dr. Woody Oakes	Studholme
Dan Kennedy	Dr. John Kois	Taki Moore
Larry Pino	Dr. Ron Sheetz	Mike Gunn
Zakiya Larry	Jared Duckett	Walter Wofford
Dr. Mike Abernathy	Bill Ladd	Marty Fort
Monica Austin	Marcus Crigler	Richard James
Grace Bunch	John Hyre	Eland Mann
Ron Sheetz	Jeffrey Watson	Darcy Juarez
Dr. Chris Griffin	Mary Hart	Mike Meeker
Bill Glazer	Dave Stech	Dr. Will Moreland

My Freedom Founders team:

Davy Tyburski	Lindsey Cope	Nathanael Brunner
Alex Lerma	Crystal Hollis	Olivia Brunner
Robert Brace	Nathan Webster	Blaine Oelkers

My amazing heroes and comrades in arms – The Members of the Freedom Founders Community!

Our co-collaborators and investment providers – The Freedom Founders Trusted Advisors!

TABLE OF CONTENTS

FOREWORD

BY DAN S. KENNEDY

Can _YOU_ Personally Direct Your Methodical Progress To _Real_, Secure Financial Freedom?

DE-_Mystification._

Money is made mysterious by an industry of money: all the Wall Street creatures and denizens, brokers, 401K and IRA "packagers" and managers, "advisors" (term used loosely), money-under-management (MUM) practitioners, insurance, annuity and other financial product manufacturers and providers, the white-shoe boys at Goldman Sachs and similar firms, etc.—_all of whom prefer you just sign on the dotted lines where they put the little sticky notes._

What I call _"the Business of YOUR money"_ is meant to be intimidating, so you just let the "professionals" attend to it for you, and you ask few questions—_not_ wanting to be embarrassed by asking a "stupid" question. My friend, famous author Robert Ringer, says THE question of life, separating winners from losers at every turn, is: _To Be_ *or NOT to Be Intimidated?* (The title of his great book.) Your progress and success has been all about first being intimidated, then working your way to NOT being intimidated—maybe about delivering case presentations and citing fees (without sweaty palms); about managing and disciplining (and when necessary, firing) staff; about every aspect of practice. That same process *has to be* applied to "the business of YOUR money."

"Personal Finance" is deliberately, intentionally enshrouded in apparent complexity in order to make you "give up" and surrender your sovereignty and authority to Them.

You *know* this. That's one of the reasons you came here, to this book. You *know* in your mind and heart that "just letting Joe do it" with YOUR money is a dangerous idea. You say to yourself: there *must* be a better way. And you are right!

There are certainly things that offer you little opportunity for control. If you need heart surgery, for example, you are NOT going to study up, stay awake, and collaborate on and supervise the operation. You will have no choice but to find the best-qualified surgeon you can get, be especially nice to him, close your eyes, say a prayer, and Let Dr. Joe Do It. But "the business of YOUR money" does NOT have to be handled this way—and we insist, shouldn't.

DE-Mystification.

The chief purpose of this book IS to de-mystify, de-intimidate, and return authority over your financial life to you, where it belongs. This includes and requires **clarifying** your own personal money goals, present and future, so that all decisions have a crystal clear, articulated governance. A guiding light visible, always, even through thick fog. This includes **simplifying** the path to true financial freedom, including full replacement of actively earned income with passive income, in as little as three to seven years.

Dr. David Phelps, the chief author of this book, is **UNIQUELY qualified** to take you on *this* path, because he has cut through the confusing and intimidating jungle to make it, taken it personally, and helped thousands of his peers – dentists, practice owners, and other small business owners – make it theirs, surefootedly and successfully.

There is a story about hired guides. Two novice hunters hire a much advertised "Best Guide Ever," a distant nephew of Davy Crockett, with an Expert Guide Certification from the International Institute of Professional Guides, to take them on their virgin hunting trip into the North Woods. About five hours into the trek, one of the novice hunters timidly pipes up, saying he believes they have hiked past the same little creek's waterfall three times. "Yes sir," says the guide. "That's because, sir, I'm afraid we are lost." The shocked hunters splutter! "How can we be lost? We hired YOU, advertised as 'the best guide ever.' Why, you're certified!" Somewhat chastened, their guide mumbles: "*But if you read the fine print,* you'll see that I'm the Best Guide Ever in Canada. We are, however, in Minnesota."

More money gets stolen each year with the fine print than with all the guns floating around. But the point is that any guide can make himself out to be the best guide—the relevant question is: is he the best guide FOR YOU? Amongst other considerations, relevant, successful experience should loom large.

Lots of people have "Guide" business cards printed up to hand to you – the "rich doctor" or "successful business owner" (prime prospect) – at cocktail parties, at exhibit booths, at

conventions, at the bank. But <u>few if any have "Done IT"—accomplished what you want to accomplish.</u> They are hardware store owners selling tools for gold mining, but they have never actually mined gold. They can be useful, carefully, narrowly delegated to, but they can also be quite dangerous. Unlike any and all of them, Dr. Phelps HAS, in fact, Done IT. Then there are the academic theorists; college professors, financial advisors, financial "pundits" Seen-On-TV. They write books, give lectures, do webinars, all *without* having Done IT. Yes, their ideas, opinions, and information CAN be instructive. One would be foolish, for example, to ignore what Warren Buffet and Charlie Munger, Jim Rogers, or Sam Zell have to say. But, still, **none have Done exactly what you want to do, starting from where you are. Dr. Phelps has. So, he UNIQUELY understands you, speaks your language, shares your experiences, and, from personal experience, knows the "Financial Freedom TRANSITION" you have to make and the way you have to make it. This is the UNIQUE perspective he has brought to this book. He *is* UNIQUELY qualified to be *your* 'DE-Mystifier-In-Chief.'**

I come from a similar perspective. Although my professional practice was in the fields of consulting, advertising copywriting, speaking, and authorship, not dentistry, it had the same underlying and severe risk factor: almost 100 percent dependence on me. A flaw finally surfaced when I was struck so ill I entered hospice to die, and was completely out of active earning and operating my business for ten months. Fortunately, long before then, I had become adept at "the Business of My Money," and even had a "machine" in place, featuring passive income, that could be safely operated on my behalf. Along the way, I'd had to decide to learn and then re-learn about "the Business of MY Money" as much as I had learned and kept learning about my other businesses. **This is THE central point of this book: getting you to take "the Business of YOUR Money" seriously, getting you as interested in it as you have been in your business's successful operation and in your technical expertise, and guiding you toward doing exactly that—as an *independent*, informed, capable, and confident thinker about your money and its uses to achieve your goals.**

Here's why getting to this point – independent, informed, CAPABLE and CONFIDENT about the Business of Your Money – is so vital. Napoleon Hill, much-celebrated author of *Think and Grow Rich*, asserted that "anything your mind can conceive *and believe*, you can achieve." You cannot achieve your financial freedom without believing that you can—with REAL belief, grounded on reason (not merely "positive thinking").

I'll share more from my experiences in my chapters in this book. For now, let me say that I think very differently about money than most "experts" you may have been hearing from throughout your career to the present. And I have made the "transition" successfully, achieving *zero* debt and *zero* need for any actively earned income to satisfy my needs and interests—which include owning racehorses (the "investment" that eats while you sleep), only flying by private planes when traveling, and generously supporting a handful of charities and organizations I deem well-operated and important. In other words, I'm *not* cheap to keep. I have "traveled" and transitioned from "high income, under-invested" (i.e., broke with more zeroes) to fully supported by investments, now continuing with some active work only by choice and with limitations imposed by my medical crises' lasting impairments. I achieved this "NO Need Position" by age fifty. In short, like David, I speak from personal experience, *not* academic theory, *not* Wall Street dogma, and *not* with my tongue-tied by having to sell something to you.

I HAVE MADE THE "TRANSITION" SUCCESSFULLY, ACHIEVING ZERO DEBT AND ZERO NEED FOR ANY ACTIVELY EARNED INCOME TO SATISFY MY NEEDS AND INTERESTS.

Let's be very clear: THIS book is profoundly different from all other books about money, investing, and personal finance. If your skepticism and disappointment with traditional, "normal," standard, common advice, investment products, and packaged ways to entrust others to produce your retirement security has been rising, you *will* find the "breath of fresh air" you're more than ready for right here, in these pages. If you are REALLY ready for it, you will even discover a true SECRET to financial and personal independence. Be on the alert!

A CALL TO ARMS

"Toto, I've a feeling we're not in Kansas anymore."

Judy Garland as Dorothy, The Wizard of Oz

"A society's worth isn't measured by how much power is seized by its government but rather how much power is reserved for its people."

Chris Salcedo, veteran television and radio
broadcaster, author, and political analyst

Why this book and why now?

The Enemies of the Republic Have Crossed the Rubicon.

America was founded in 1776 on the blood, sweat, and tears of our founding fathers and the host of other colonists who fought to break ranks from the tyranny of the King of England. That America is losing its freedom at a very fast pace.

Today, few of us feel truly free, limited as we are by "circumstances" and "responsibilities."

Even fewer can say, "I own my freedom." Why?

Fifty years ago, this country was fighting communists. Today, we have elected them into public office with open arms. We are welcoming the fox into the hen house, gullibly believing assurances that it is for our own good and for the good of the vulnerable among us. Don't for a moment trust the "good" intentions of the powerful voices who are leading us toward the cliff. The "generosity" they offer to the masses will certainly create dependency and propagate a larger and larger welfare system.

Dependency = Control. True totalitarian power cannot reign in a society where personal freedom and autonomy exist. In order to achieve complete power, personal freedom must be undermined, restricted, and ultimately eliminated.

Political and economic unrest is not new to the world. Plagues and disease are well-described in history books. During volatile times, there are winners and losers. Those who are resilient and adaptable survive—and, quite often, thrive.

What Got You Here Won't Get You Where You Want To Go.

Whatever you've done so far – going to school, studying and working hard, achieving and maintaining your licensure, building and acquiring your practice or business, enduring the risk and liability you take every single day as a practitioner and small business owner, the weekly grind "putting in the hours" to create stability and security for your family – isn't enough, because everything you have worked so hard for is at risk.

Everything you have worked so hard for is at risk.

My co-author and mentor, Dan S. Kennedy, has lived his own life based on his number one principle: *personal sovereignty*, which can be described as individual freedom. I have learned much from his teachings, and have employed many of his principles of autonomy in my own life. Dan is not apologetic in any way for preserving his right to choose—how he lives, where he lives, who he allows into his personal and work life, and how his time is governed.

You should enact similar principles *if* you value your freedom. This book was written with that goal in mind. Don't simply read this book and place it on your bookshelf. Take action. Failure to do so may severely limit your options in the future.

You might ask, *Is it too late to change course?* To quote the words of the wise economist (and national treasure) Thomas Sowell: "Nothing is irreversible, but when we are completely unwilling to do what needs to be done, it is inevitable."

Do we have the collective will as a nation to change course? You and I might, but I doubt that the hordes of young people marching out the doors of today's public schools into the real world of working, voting, bill-paying, saving, investing, and business-growing do.

In fact, they appear hell-bent on running toward the cliff faster than ever. According to a 2019 Gallup survey socialism is equally as popular as capitalism among U.S. young adults.[1]

---

1 Lydia Saad, "Socialism as Popular as Capitalism Among Young Adults in U.S.," Gallup, November, 25, 2019, https://news.gallup.com/poll/268766/socialism-popular-capitalism-among-young-adults.aspx

We've come a long way from the cloudy day when Reagan stood at the Brandenburg gate in West Berlin and shouted, "Mr. Gorbachev, tear down this wall!"

The Question for Each of Us: What Will You Do About It?

This is NOT a time to put your head in the sand. What brought you this far is not to be relied upon in this brave new world. Now is not a time to rely on old formulas and traditions:

★ A degree/license guaranteeing economic independence

★ "Work hard, pay taxes, and save"

★ 401(k)s, cash balance plans, and other traditional tax deferral strategies (do any of us really believe taxes will go down in the future?)

Those outdated models will no longer be the "golden ticket" they once were. In fact, they may be the WORST thing you could do right now. Don't follow the majority. Relying on your ability to earn income and playing the tax "deferral" game is playing the game by yesterday's rules.

Your conventional advisors – your CPA, financial advisor, business or estate planning attorney, or 401(k) administrator – are not in any position to help you. They are too busy in the day-to-day work of their profession, putting out the fires and making a living (just like you are). They are still operating in yesterday's "normal." They are not prepared for what's coming.

You need a better plan—a plan based on where we're headed, not where we've been.

Step One: Preserve your Freedom.
Put *your* oxygen mask on first.

I talk to business and practice owners on a regular basis who have two primary concerns. One: they want a pathway to their own personal Freedom, to get off the treadmill (because right now it looks very bleak for many of them). They don't see a path to the financial security they desire. Second: Just about every one of them wants to do more to better prepare their kids or grandkids for the future.

The problem? Most owners don't have a plan to accomplish either of these mandates—for themselves or for future generations. This is no way to live a life, and it's no way to prepare your family for the future.

If you're a licensed business in a highly regulated arena (such as healthcare, financial services, etc.), you are at great risk. Because you are licensed by the state, the state has the ability to control how you do business. This is already happened in New York, where dentists are being forced into a single payer system where they must see patients who are receiving "free" healthcare.

My advice? Put your oxygen mask on first.

★ Do the hard work of becoming financially independent from the need to generate earned income from your business. This will free you from the state's ability to hold you hostage.

★ Create real, sustainable cash-flow streams outside your business. These income streams can be relied upon to provide for yourself and your family even during times of economic turbulence. (How many of us imagined that we would be shut down by government mandate due to a global pandemic?)

★ Secure your wealth with real, tangible assets (not financial "paper" assets). I prefer assets that are producing sustainable, predictable cash flow regardless of the ups and downs of the markets.

★ Limit your exposure to government-controlled "retirement" plans such as 401(k)s. These plans force you to surrender control of your wealth. And trust me, the government is able and willing to change the rules to exert control when they deem it necessary "for the greater good."

The renewed rise of socialism is a call to action for the rest of us. If we want to maintain and protect our freedom, we must first preserve our own so that we can in turn help others.

Preserving your own autonomy is the first step.

> # If we want to maintain and protect our freedom, we must first preserve our own so that we can in turn help others.

Step Two: A plan to preserve liberty for future generations.

Your autonomy is just the beginning. What about our kids? The next generation is facing an existential threat to the liberties we have known and enjoyed in our lifetime.

How are you preparing them to face an uncertain future? Hint: If you're thinking that simply leaving a pile of money to your kids will be the answer, it's NOT. In fact, that might be the worst thing you could do for your kids UNLESS you are also teaching them the principles by which to obviate this move toward socialism. Giving an adult child a pile of money they didn't earn without teaching them the principles that created that wealth in the first place is like letting a toddler drive a sports car—nothing good will happen.

Many of my well-meaning colleagues will leave significant amounts of wealth to children who are not prepared to preserve and grow it and who may actually use that wealth to support causes that actively undermine the principles that created the wealth in the first place.

If you have children, young or in adulthood, you must teach them to be resourceful and to actively counteract the indoctrination they are receiving every day from school, teachers, coaches, mentors, and peers. Expose them to voices who actually understand economics (such as the above-quoted Thomas Sowell). Challenge them and lead by example. If possible, plug them into peer groups or a tribe that will guide them in the right direction.

Most of all, don't try to "go it alone."

You need a place where there is truth, wisdom, and experience. You need deep connections in a network of like-minded people who share your values. No one has a crystal ball. We can't predict exactly when or where these changes will take place. But whatever happens, it must not be faced alone.

Me?

I'm not afraid.

I have surrounded myself with a tribe of smart, seasoned, freedom-loving people who share my core values and believe in the things that I believe. They are committed to preserving and expanding wealth (and with it freedom and autonomy, the very things that are at risk right now).

Together, we can navigate whatever the future holds.

What about you? Are you confident that your plan and tribe will enable you to be successful in an uncertain future? The clock is ticking. It's time to get your house in order. To quote Margaret Thatcher:

"Marxists get up early in the morning to further their cause. We must get up even earlier to defend our freedom."

This book is for young people looking ahead, for those mid-career rethinking where they are on the path forward, for veteran entrepreneurs and investors, and for fiscal conservatives, who want to get off the hamster wheel and start owning their freedom.

This is a wake-up call. Don't sleep through the alarm!

We live in a capitalist society. How are you going to play? How will you participate? There is no time or place for bystanders or those who would rather wait and watch.

Do I resist changing, just play it safe, and hope for a return to normal? Do I depend on the government or my industry's lobbying efforts to bring justice and "make it fair?"

No. To create sustainability through the forthcoming bedlam, you must be a renegade, not by protesting in the streets nor by crying foul when government, taxation, or regulation appears to tie your hands. No—being a renegade means going in a different direction.

Don't follow the majority. This is no time to be placid. Fight for your autonomy. We must bring freedom back to each of us as individuals. This is where it has to start. Value your freedom. Don't take it for granted. Don't leave it up to others.

Every action you take must be based on a guiding principle, philosophy, or concept. This is about what you stand for, what you believe, your convictions; where you draw the line, or your non-negotiables. If you aren't clear in this regard, then you are only flailing away chasing silver bullets or bright shiny objects. Don't be like the majority, who have no clue and are constantly distracted by "new and promising."

How does one become clear and focused on a guiding principle? You question everyone and everything, even your own limiting beliefs.

You do this by looking twice at what you read, watch, and to whom you listen. In other words, the environment in which you place yourself is critical. Who you spend time with is a factor that many grossly overlook (see Jim Rohn's quote: "You are the average of the five people you spend the most time with").

I've intentionally invested in my network, what I call *relationship capital,* because I see these relationships as an investment in my freedom. I don't want to be the smartest one in the room (that's the wrong room). Ego is not my driver. Constant reality checks and accountability from a network or community of people who I can count on for the harsh truth, who force me to ask better questions, are what lifts me up. I can say with conviction that, while my life is not without challenges, resets, and redos, my ability to stay on course and pivot as needed is at least 10X the capabilities of my earlier years.

You are the most valuable asset in your portfolio. Know your freedom and personal sovereignty is more valuable than gold.

> *You* are the most valuable asset in your portfolio. Know your freedom and personal sovereignty is more valuable than gold.

It's a pay-to-play world. I invest annually well into six figures in my personal coaching, mentoring, and mastermind communities. As a side benefit, the government picks up 40 percent-plus on the tab for that investment (business and/or investment expense). As soon as you think you know it all and don't need anyone else to test your thinking and actions, you're done. Failure is imminent at some level. Personal coaching can be a very humbling experience. But don't give up on your freedom.

The bottom line: It will be tough sledding ahead for a broad swath of the American population. It is critical for those who you care for to understand that the forces at play are not working in their favor.

Freedom is not easy. It requires vigilance and sacrifice. In our country, the freedom to make these decisions is key to who we are as Americans. Going forward we must persevere, remain resolute, and push away our fears to protect our freedoms. My call to arms is, "Own Your Freedom."

If you don't, someone else will.

PART I

WHY OWN YOUR YOUR FREEDOM?

"In the truest sense, freedom cannot be bestowed; it must be achieved."

President Franklin D. Roosevelt

CHAPTER 1

DO YOU OWN YOUR FREEDOM?

BY DR. DAVID PHELPS

"Those who would give up essential Liberty,
to purchase a little temporary Safety,
deserve neither Liberty nor Safety."

Benjamin Franklin

ew of us are truly free. Even in the United States, freedom isn't something we inherit or enjoy just because we are Americans. To enjoy freedom, we have to work for it. We have to work for freedom as a group. And we have to work for freedom as individuals. Freedom takes work, no doubt. But the question you must ask is: what *type* of work achieves *your* freedom?

FREEDOM QUESTIONS

....

How *free* do you feel? How confident are you
in your next paycheck? How many hours in
the day are you trading for dollars? Do you do
what you want, when you want, and still have
the money needed for your life and future?

Dr. Greg Winstead worked most of his life *thinking* he was working
toward freedom. Then, suddenly, as the Covid-19 pandemic closed
businesses, yanked the rug from under the stock market, and dropped
the economy into a recession, Greg realized the truth. I share his story
because it's similar to mine and that of many professionals I've worked
with over the years. Maybe you, too, can relate to his story.

In March 2020, at the outset of the Covid-19 pandemic, I
received a call from Dr. Greg.

"David," he said, "they're shutting us down." Alarm was in his voice.

You see, Greg had spent the past two decades fighting tooth
and nail to build a successful dental practice in New York City.
After opening the doors in his thirties, Dr. Greg earned a pristine
reputation and loyal clientele by working the long hours it took to get
the business off the ground.

This meant that Greg made sacrifices at home. He left the house
early and arrived home late. He didn't see his kids as often as he
would've liked. And he wasn't the partner he wanted to be for his
wife, Phyllis.

On the business side, despite the practice's success, Greg knew
he was struggling. He was making payments on a loan. He had credit

card debt that wasn't going down. And while he was putting money into his 401(k), he was already 52 years old, and the nest egg seemed smaller than what he wished it would be.

Worst of all, even though Greg had an accomplished staff of ten professionals, he felt like he was struggling *alone*.

Greg isn't a complainer. It's his nature to do a great job, be the best he can be, and not sweat the small stuff. But if you were to prod, he'd tell you his back was killing him, from being hunched over half the day for twenty-plus years. He regretted buying a second relatively expensive car instead of an economy model. And maybe he'd even tell you what he told me the second time we spoke—that sometimes, he feels "trapped." Trapped by debt, by a more-than-modest lifestyle, by the advice from Wall Street that never seemed to work out as he expected, and by the responsibility of shouldering his business all these years.

Most of all, Greg felt trapped by the *work*. He couldn't do what he wanted, with whom he wanted, where he wanted, how he wanted, and when he wanted. Instead, most nights after a big day at the office, he'd lie awake and wonder: "Is this the best way?" He was a hard-charging entrepreneur, sure—but did he need to *be or do something else?*

Then, Greg's situation got much worse.

Covid-19 surprised him like it did many business owners. One day, Greg was welcoming twenty patients into his office, discussing with them their issues and how he could help. The next day, the business was closed indefinitely. No more customers, no more money. If only the bills went away, too!

Thankfully, Greg had made a few key changes to his business, lifestyle, and budget over the previous year.

You see, in 2019, Greg had made the decision to *rework* how he was working. He wanted to stop trading his time for dollars, to start working toward freedom. He wanted to get to a place where he could do what he wanted when he wanted. Where he could spend more time with his family. Where his back didn't hurt so much.

For many professionals like Greg, that means a transition from working a *job* to becoming an *owner*. Not just a business owner, but an owner of real estate and other investments that can generate income. These assets provide cash flow, so they earn you more money than just what's in your paycheck.

These assets provide cash flow, so they earn you more money than just what's in your paycheck.

When Greg called me, alarmed at the beginning of the pandemic, we discussed how much better prepared he was in 2020 than he'd been in 2019.

"Greg," I said, "your business is taking a hit. You can forget about the income from that. Now's the time to live within the cash flow you've established from your other assets."

A few weeks later, in April 2020, Greg and I spoke with a group of other socially distancing entrepreneurs from around the US in a Zoom call. Greg was one of the many assembled who was thankful to have set up secondary forms of income. With their primary businesses around the country shuttered for two months, these entrepreneurs were staying afloat *on passive cash flow from real estate interests they owned.*

These entrepreneurs had been working toward this position for a year-plus. Before the pandemic, they had started investing in assets as a way to eventually work less in their primary job. But then, as the pandemic dragged on, these entrepreneurs realized the most powerful truth of income generated from owned property: their wealth worked for them, no matter the external economic conditions.

"We're so thankful that our wealth is now sustainable," said one entrepreneur.

"We have more choices than we would've a year ago," said another.

It made me wonder. "Despite the economic volatility," I asked, "do you feel like you own your freedom?"

"Yes," was the unanimous response.

Imagine that. Entrepreneurs, whose businesses were closed, yet were still making money from multiple streams of income. They weren't trading time for dollars to earn active income. They were just earning passive income by *owning assets that others paid to use.*

Most important? These were not people who had $5 million cash in the bank. Far from it. These were people who owned a business and investments in real estate assets. Some had at most $2 million in *equity*—not liquid cash—which they'd earned after working decades to pay off a home or two. What's remarkable is not that they owned these assets but that they were using the assets to generate multiple streams of income *even during the worst of the pandemic.*

I was thrilled for them. Not least because of their sustainable wealth. But, somewhat selfishly, I was thrilled because I'd always had a hunch: *there is a better way,* and it's one that works in both good and bad times.

For years, I've believed in the power of ownership to generate passive or annuity income. I built a life and livelihood in pursuit of freedom through this passive income.

My belief and livelihood have been tested before—during the 2001 dot-com bubble burst and again in the 2008-2009 housing crisis and Great Recession. But it wasn't until the 2020 Covid-19 pandemic that we faced our biggest, truest test. Could our approach to work and wealth survive the pandemic and any economic volatility that followed?

Could our approach to work and wealth survive the pandemic and any economic volatility that followed?

The results were better than I ever dreamed: Not only did our approach survive, but it passed with flying colors.

2020 was a devastating year for many people and businesses. Hundreds of thousands sick and many who died as a result of the pandemic. Millions lost jobs and struggled to put food on the table. Small business entrepreneurs everywhere faced tough decisions. Which bills do I pay this month? Do I let people go? Do I close shop? Do I give up on the dream? Thousands of entrepreneurs were trapped by these decisions. Many didn't survive.

But, even in the best of times, many entrepreneurs feel trapped, torn by different needs, as did Greg, who had the "Covid Wake-Up Call," and wondered:

★ Do I work harder and longer, and try to *save* more, so I can possibly retire before it's too late?

★ Or do I work less and spend more time with my family now, even though I may be aching all over before I can retire?

These questions are two sides of a false choice. *Neither* question can give you an answer that helps you achieve freedom.

So, when questioning your approach to work and your livelihood, start by asking a question about your freedom.

The big freedom question we ask in this chapter and in this book: *What type of work achieves your truest freedom?*

What Is Freedom?

Before we answer what type of work achieves our truest freedom, let's first understand more about freedom.

We live in the United States of America, where our government has enshrined into law our freedoms as a people. Freedom is our right as Americans. That said, we know "freedom ain't free"—it's a privilege that generations of Americans and all those who've served have fought to earn for us. We thank them.

But what about our freedom on an individual level? Is our individual freedom something we also must fight for?

The short answer is yes. As an individual, your freedom is in your hands. It's a beautiful truth. Especially because, in our world, most everything else is outside of our control.

Think about it. We don't have direct control over our environment, politics, or economy. When Wall Street crashes because of a mortgage crisis, we lament those who did it, but we don't feel much personal accountability. When the pandemic response shutters our business, we're upset, but there's no "instant button" we can push to undo the government's decision. We don't have control over these larger national or global forces.

Thankfully, the best thing in the world is entirely in our control: our own personal sovereignty. And with personal sovereignty, we can always choose our path to personal freedom.

Freedom is a condition in which people have the opportunity to speak, act, and pursue happiness without unnecessary external restrictions. The true meaning of freedom lies in the rightful execution of your rights and letting others do the same.

In other words: *freedom means you take ownership of your actions.* That's it. Freedom is ownership of your choices, what you choose to do. It's as simple as that.

> *Freedom means you take ownership of your actions.* That's it. Freedom is ownership of your choices, what you choose to do.

That's why I titled this book, *Own Your Freedom*. Because freedom is something you *must* own. If not *you*, then someone else will.

When you own your freedom, you choose how, where, and why to spend your time and money. You are doing *what* you enjoy doing (your work or hobby, etc.), *where* you want to do it, with *whom* you want to do it (clients, patients, colleagues, family, friends, etc.), *when* you want to do it, and *how* you want to do it. If this condition doesn't describe you, then your freedom is at risk.

We don't own our freedom by default. It's something we always— each of us—must work for if we want it. The important part is that we have to know the difference between freedom and security. Most of us work for more and more security and, as a result, often sacrifice the freedom we really want.

Think back to the story of Dr. Greg Winstead. During his first two decades in business, he had been working for more and more security.

He took the traditional default retirement plan by saving money in a 401(k) that couldn't provide cash flow until he was nearly sixty years old, sacrificing his back—and his family life—in the process.

When I started working with Greg in 2019, I could hear it in his every word—*he craved freedom*. Yet he was chasing the opposite: security without a plan.

If you're reading this book, odds are that you aren't as free as you could be. You likely feel trapped by the false sense of security you've pursued, and are looking for better choices to help you establish sustainable wealth so that you can own your freedom.

The pursuit of security is common to us. Whether you're a student, a professional, an entrepreneur, or anyone else, we need a degree of security to function. But with too much focus on security, we put our freedom at risk. It happens to all of us. We just have to be aware of the risks—the threats and traps that limit our freedom—so we can truly start owning our freedom.

Your Freedom Is at Risk

Personal sovereignty is a double-edged sword. We can choose freedom. Or, we can choose security. Most of us seek some combination of both.

The trouble is, security *restricts* freedom. We may willingly choose security—for example, trading time for dollars working a passionless job, so we can buy food for our family—but choosing security doesn't make us feel any *freer*. On top of that, the premise of "security" is often false, if our security is dependent on a situation that could be destroyed in one economic recession, pandemic, or personal crisis.

Security is necessary. We need to be able to buy food. But our goal should be to have food *and* freedom. And not a little food or freedom, but plenty—enough so you don't feel trapped or torn by competing priorities. All *without* sacrificing your freedom.

I'll say the important part again: Your goal is to enjoy and sustain as much freedom as you can, as soon as you can.

Your goal is to enjoy and sustain as much freedom as you can, as soon as you can.

While freedom means owning your actions and having more choices, few of us choose to own our actions or find more choices. That means we've put our freedom at risk. It's nobody's fault, but there is plenty we can do to protect our freedom from these risks, as long as you know how they are limiting your freedom in the first place.

What about you? How are you protecting your freedom?
- ★ *Did your investments take a hit during the Covid-19 downturn?*
- ★ *What are you doing to hedge against future government-mandated shutdowns, regulations, restrictions, or other external events that directly affect your livelihood and ability to trade time for dollars?*
- ★ *Do you have a plan for acquiring real tangible assets (not Wall Street stocks and bonds) that will produce recurring monthly cash flow with a hedge against inflation and ultimately replace your requirement to work?*
- ★ *Do you wish you had more time for what matters most to you?*
- ★ *What is your game plan to achieve financial freedom?*
- ★ *What puts your freedom at risk?*

In my discussions over the years with entrepreneurs of all stripes, we've defined six main threats to freedom. To understand how these threats relate to our freedom, we ask: *Are you...*

1. *Stuck on Active Income?*
2. *Locked into Wall Street-first Advice?*
3. *Trapped by Debt and Expectations?*
4. *Dependent on Government?*
5. *Limited by Going It Alone?*

Let's unpack each of these threats.

1. Stuck on Active Income?

Active income is where most of us start. Unless you're a trust fund baby!

We've all had jobs—especially through school and into our early careers—that we worked just to pay for the cost of living.

But the goal should be to transition from current income to future bank—our wealth, equity, net worth—by *building it as quickly as you can* from the proceeds of your active income.

This wealth can be used to generate passive income, which means you're getting paid without having to show up every day. Sounds great, right? But few of us actually do it.

Most of us get stuck on active income. We get into a career track thinking we have to ride it to the end of the line. That can be a bumpy ride, especially considering the regular volatility of the economy, the threat of more government interference, and higher rates of taxation and confiscation of our money.

Reducing one's reliance on active income is difficult because it is not the norm. We are taught through years of education to become skilled workers; the higher the skill, the greater the potential income. Going against the grain, against societal and industry "standards," is not easy. But this is about *your* freedom—if you live by the agendas of others, your freedom will prove to be forever elusive.

Your willingness and ability to pivot or make significant changes when needed are key to the preservation of your freedom. If you're an entrepreneur, you may already be adaptable or at least comfortable with flexibility. But many other professionals—for example, those who spend years in academia earning a graduate degree—usually aren't as adaptable as they need to be. They're stuck in one career, which means they're stuck on active income.

A long career focused on a single industry or profession is a very difficult way to achieve freedom. It's not even a model that guarantees security anymore. Spending years and years pursuing formal, specialized education isn't the "sure investment" it was a few decades ago, so today we must balance it with self-education and other business endeavors, especially the development of secondary and passive income.

We'll talk more about how to replace active income with other assets to hit your *Freedom Number*, a concept we introduce in chapter 2. But rest assured, you achieve freedom when you've got cash flow (or annuity) that doesn't rely on your active, transactional income.

2. Locked into Wall Street-first Advice?

Wall Street's standard financial planning model works best for Wall Street. It's based on tax-deferral through third-party managed 401(k) plans, defined benefit, and cash balance plans invested in the stock market. Does that always work best for you? Or does it just tie up your money in assets you can't touch?

Think about it. This planning model removes the ability for you, a business owner, to have any control over these funds—and worse, no access to the capital until age 59.5. Following such a model is an abdication of your financial future. Just because this risk has been accepted by the majority in our society doesn't mean you have to do it too.

Aside from putting your money in Wall Street and "letting it ride," especially in volatile times, there's not much other advice you'll find in the industry. That's because the entire Wall Street machine is built on the concept of accumulation, and accumulation is neither ownership nor freedom. It is a model rife with uncertainty.

Accumulation is neither ownership nor freedom.

In our Freedom Founders meetings, when I discuss with our members the advice they receive from their financial advisors – all of whom follow the Wall Street accumulation model – they report the advisors recommend for high-income earners an accumulation of $6 million to $10 million before retirement. Why so much? Because this model doesn't generate passive cash flow. And because the advisor moves the investments to "safe and conservative" bonds, annuities, or CDs, the retiree is forced to deplete the accumulated principal over the remainder of their life, with the hope that the money outlasts them.

Say again?

Even with high-income earners, not many can accumulate a retirement nest egg in the realm of $6 million to $10 million. And that is the reason that so many hard-working professionals and business owners feel compelled to continue grinding it out past age 60, 65, or even into their 70s, which is not all that uncommon today. "I'll never retire!" is the common refrain, because, for the majority, they're stuck in a broken and flawed financial model. Financial acumen is not taught in schools or universities. Even those with financial degrees don't study the concepts presented in this book.

Thankfully, there is an alternative path to financial freedom. However, very few understand it and fewer still are able to implement this approach because of a few key concepts that are missing.

One might wonder: *Why doesn't the traditional financial advisor community recommend real estate or alternative investments as an investment vehicle?*

Over the years, I've discovered a few answers:

* Financial planners don't make money (fees or commissions) from real estate.
* Financial planners don't understand the benefits of real estate, because their industry is built on the accumulation of assets on Wall Street.
* Real estate is an "inefficient" market, which means that accessing it and selling it is not as scalable as selling Wall Street products.
* Wall Street is a major marketing engine that has indoctrinated the majority into thinking that financial products are the means to economic independence.

3. Trapped by Debt and Expectations?

Many of us desire to live a well-off lifestyle—not just to be with our family and put food on our table, but more. Much more.

Big house. Fast car. The best colleges for our kids. It's still all about keeping up with the Joneses, even if we now do the keeping up on Instagram or Facebook.

And herein lies one of the fatal flaws of high-income earners – making money becomes a trap in itself. How? More income equates to an elevated lifestyle because that is what is expected of those who are well-educated and work hard.

I have no issue or judgment about anyone's choice of lifestyle. I do know that putting lifestyle *first* without regard to an income-replacement plan (passive or annuity income based on tangible assets) is a road to working longer, harder, and with more frustration and burnout.

Funding such a lifestyle can get expensive, fast. I know many otherwise well-off professionals who are burdened by high consumption debt, typically from credit cards. Sure, they may have a respectable career and earn $200 or more an hour, but they also have $50,000 in credit card debt. Did any of that money go toward their freedom? Or was it toward a luxury item they wanted?

It is not uncommon for me to have a conversation with a mid-career, fifty-something doctor or business owner who has by society's standards been successful in career, family, and lifestyle. But success is not the focus of the conversation. No. It's about, "Where does this go? Where's my endpoint? How do I exit this treadmill?"

By this point in their career, the doctor thought that they'd be over the hump. That, by now, his or her practice or business would be serviced by junior associates or partners, that their work time "in" the business would be far reduced, and that money problems would not exist.

This predicament is in fact so common that the majority of the business owners with whom I consult between the ages of 55 and 65 have $2 million in assets, including retirement accounts, after-tax investments, personal residence, or other real estate and their perceived (fingers-crossed) business equity. In addition, most are still paying mortgages on the big house and have multiple auto loans or leases. Some are unfortunately still dealing with the financial beating of a prior divorce (sometimes multiple).

There are plenty of ways to spend your money. However, few are an investment that *strengthens* your freedom. Most are a trap, offering a false sense of security in exchange for debt. Be warned that consumption debt and the misguided expectations of society do little to help you own your freedom.

4. Dependent on Government (or the Capital of Others)?

Our country was built on the foundation of capitalism. Don't let the current media distort the true meaning and societal benefits of capitalism. It's not a perfect model, but, then again, no other model has produced a country and society as vibrant as ours. While we live in the midst of a major transitional shift toward socialism, historically our society and government are organized to support capital and those who own it.

If you don't own any capital, then you are missing out on one of our society's fundamental organizing principles. Make no mistake, our government largesse and crony capitalism have created and continue to create greater wealth inequality. This is not true capitalism. This is an external factor over which you and I have no direct control. Therefore, not understanding how to acquire and amass capital (primarily in alternative investments) works to the detriment of your freedom and sustainable wealth.

Today, when we look at inequality trends, the middle class is shrinking, and the rich are getting richer. The share of capital is in fewer and fewer hands, and I agree this is a problem. But if you want to maintain your freedom and the ability to have a positive impact on the freedoms of others, you must learn how to achieve and maintain that freedom for yourself first. I often say, "This is a time to put your oxygen mask on first." Only then are you in a position to help others.

In search of a solution, some people consider "socialism" or socialist policies, where the government provides "safety nets" through massive entitlement programs and corporate and Wall Street bailouts. This is government "taking advantage of a crisis" and using a crisis to create more dependence on the government, thereby reducing and restraining the freedom of the people. Remember our discussion about the "trade of liberty for perceived security?" This is the plan for more control by the political elites. It is your responsibility *not* to allow your security and livelihood to be dependent on the promises of the government.

To do otherwise is a mistake that too many have already made. Overall, I think socialism is missing the point. Sure, we all benefit from social benefits such as Social Security, Medicare for our elders, and other government programs. But to think that the government— which is really just the capital of others—will provide your individual freedom is a mistake. Remember, if you don't own your freedom, then someone else will.

Capitalism isn't the issue—we don't throw the baby out with the bathwater. The issue is a matter of participation. More and more people need to own capital. When more of us rely on government, then capital gets concentrated into fewer and fewer hands. Furthermore, it disincentivizes personal responsibility and increases dependency. It's in large part the reason behind why the trend of wealth inequality continues to worsen.

The good news is that if you're a working professional, there's no reason why you can't participate in capitalism by owning property and other assets. Few workers see it that way. And that's a trap that makes you dependent on government or the capital of others.

If you're not working toward owning or controlling capital assets, then you're just half-participating in our capitalist system. You're participating as merely a worker and not an owner. Participate as an owner, and you get all the advantages that come along with it.

> # If you're not working toward owning or controlling capital assets, then you're just half-participating in our capitalist system.

If you want more people to have capital, we don't need to overhaul our system and beliefs. We just need more people to learn how to own wealth. Including you.

5. Limited by Going It Alone?

Some business owners I worked with interpreted "individual freedom" to mean "isolation." The stereotypical John Wayne rugged individualist. *Nobody helps me, and I don't help anyone else.* After working with hundreds of entrepreneurs in pursuing freedom, I believe this interpretation is a mistake.

Just because you're autonomous and independent doesn't mean you have to be lonely. In fact, going it alone is one of the *worst* approaches you can take.

If you're working alone, you will expend so much more time and experience far more headaches in just learning the basics. A community can provide you wisdom and experience, so you can get the information and support you need without the usual runaround to find the best advice. Why reinvent the wheel when someone else has a proven model waiting for you to adapt to your own personal goals and definition of freedom?

If there's one thing I've learned over the years, it's to seek out a tribe of those you trust. I'm always talking with my tribe, which includes my spouse, Kandace, friends, and mentors, such as co-author Dan Kennedy, industry colleagues, and my group of hardworking members and Trusted Advisors of Freedom Founders.

If you trust in a tribe that understands and prioritizes your freedom, they'll help you become less dependent on external forces. We can learn a lot from the path to independence that others have taken. And once you've walked it, you can help others do the same.

Take my Retirement Scorecard Assessment and in a few minutes you'll better understand where you're at and what steps you need to take to achieve your freedom.
Visit www.OwnYourFreedomBook.com/Resources

From Crisis to Freedom: My Journey

Study hard. Work harder. Save in the bank. Accumulate wealth the Wall Street way. Work hard some more. That is the approach for the majority— and I maintain it's a flawed and failed model.

I'm very typical of many of the small business owners and entrepreneurs that we speak to, in that we are all driven. It's just part of our DNA. We keep going, no matter what. We don't stop to ask for directions when we should.

We want most of all to be protective of our families. That means financial security is the number one thing we feel we need to maintain. In other words, we are driven to provide security. That described me early in my career. But how much room does that leave for our freedom?

I was brought up in a household where working hard, doing good, and aspiring to achieve was always present. It wasn't pressured upon me explicitly, it was just that both my parents were diligent, disciplined, and responsible. From a young age, I did what my elders and community expected of me.

After I graduated from dental school, I married my then sweetheart, who I had been dating for two years. We made our home and worked in our respective career paths.

Before our daughter Jenna (Jennifer) was born, I worked hard to get the practice up and running. While practicing, I also continued learning the technical side of the profession.

Then—crisis.

But my particular crisis wasn't 9/11 or the 2008 recession or Covid-19. It was a personal crisis.

One day, when Jenna was two and a half years old, she exhibited signs of fatigue and lethargy, totally out of the ordinary. After running several tests, the pediatrician's diagnosis was devastating: *acute lymphocytic leukemia.*

A three-year battle ensued, in which Jenna fought the cancer and endured chemotherapy. The chemotherapy depleted her immune system, often leading to spiking fevers that we couldn't let go untreated. We'd then take her to the hospital immediately. This happened on a regular basis. We were back and forth to the hospital, where Jenna's mom would spend days, sometimes weeks with her. Meanwhile, I'd go back to work, to provide for the family's finances.

Jenna survived that horrific experience, but my marriage did not. So much focus and emotional and physical energy were drained in looking out for Jennifer's wellbeing that nothing was left for the marriage.

Unfortunately, the worst of Jenna's illness wasn't behind us.

A couple of years after chemotherapy, Jenna started having epileptic seizures. Then, at twelve years old, she was diagnosed with end-stage liver failure.

That was another big shock. The doctors told us all the chemotherapy and anti-seizure medications she'd been given were too toxic for her liver. Without a new liver, her life would be unsustainable.

I immediately went into my normal pattern, driven as I am to provide security. I thought, "Okay, I'm going to fix this," which meant contacting all the people I knew in the medical community to find the best place for a child to have a liver transplant, which at that time happened to be in Houston.

About three months later, we got the call from the transplant coordinator at Texas Children's Hospital: "Great news, Dr. Phelps. We have a liver for Jenna!" *Life. The clock was ticking.*

The bags already packed, Jenna got picked up from school and flew to Houston with her mother, while I drove with great angst down from Dallas.

At the same time this was happening, another child who passed away in a car accident was having her organs harvested with care and concern by the transplant team doctors in Houston. Because of the beautiful gift that young girl and her parents allowed to happen, Jenna was the recipient of the liver.

As Jenna spent the next three months recovering in the children's hospital, I spent every moment I could at her bedside. I watched her struggle to breathe. I watched her work hard to overcome the immediacy of the transplant, all the changes that were going on in her body, and all the drugs she was having to take to make the transplant successful.

It was here, beside her in the hospital room, where I had more time than ever before to reflect on the past ten years of my life.

> ## It was here, beside her in the hospital room, where I had more time than ever before to reflect on the past ten years of my life.

Despite my best efforts, nothing had gone "according to plan." *Jenna's illness. Divorce. My working 'round the clock.*

And yet, Jenna was still here, beside me. I was still her father. And if I had failed personally and professionally before, I was still hopeful. I could do better for us, starting now.

What should I do? Who should I be? What do I want?

These were the questions I asked myself. Serious questions. Potentially life-changing questions. I had a hunch that the answers would require me to take a new approach and be a very different person than who I'd been.

I knew I could do it. I *had* to do it. *But how?*

Ever since graduating dental school, rather than saving my money in a bank or giving it to Wall Street, I'd been investing in real estate. By 2004, I'd accumulated thirty-five properties, the majority of which I owned debt-free.

> ## By 2004, I'd accumulated thirty-five properties, the majority of which I owned debt-free.

I faced a dilemma. *Do I have enough to not work full time?*

To find the answer, I had to make some calculations—but not complex calculations. I also considered the sale of my dental practice, which could provide additional equity I could invest. I also looked at my current real estate assets, calculating how much net cash flow these currently provided.

If I combined the two, knowing what I know about how to take equity capital and turn it into regular predictable cash flow, would I have enough from my real estate assets that I already built up, plus what would come out of the practice?

Would I have enough to provide for my family?

There in the hospital room with Jenna, I made the decision to sell my practice, stop actively producing income, and rely on passive cash flow from real estate. I would do my part in giving her the best shot at a future as possible.

I didn't know it at the time, but I was desperately searching for my Freedom Number.

Out of this struggle to calculate "enough," I arrived at the first principle, described in this chapter.

Every business owner dreams of becoming financially independent. The good news is that the more capital and equity you accumulate and the better you learn to orchestrate predictable cash-flow returns from that equity, the more likely you are to own your freedom. Notice that in my calculations to determine if I had enough, I didn't look at things like "cash in the bank" or "investments on Wall Street." I knew how to make my money (capital equity) work for me at least as hard as I worked for it.

> The better you learn to orchestrate predictable cash-flow returns from that equity, the more likely you are to own your freedom.

The path to owning your freedom starts with what you own. You don't even have to start with any assets (let alone owning thirty-five properties, as I did). Knowing how much is "enough" starts with YOUR Freedom Number. The next step is to reverse engineer the number to determine "how much equity" you need at a specific return to reach your Freedom Number. *This* is how we can reach freedom—not at a retirement age of 65, but decades earlier.

Economic Freedom & "Free for Life™"

"Economic freedom" is one of my five freedoms, along with time, relationships, health, and purpose/legacy.

When somebody has economic freedom, they're not subject to having to "go to work," whether that's a job or their own business. They have the flexibility of time. This doesn't necessarily mean they're not working or not making money doing something they enjoy. They could be doing both. It just means they don't *have* to do either. They have the flexibility to not work. They've achieved economic freedom because all their lifestyle needs are already met with annuity cash flow from real assets.

Until you reach the point where your family's lifestyle needs are met, then you are compelled to some degree to trade your time for dollars.

At the same time, your goal in trading time for dollars should be to own your freedom. Our Freedom Founders community members call this "Free for Life™." That's when you've replaced your need for active income with other assets that produce income not dependent upon you.

We also add a "safe harbor" cushion. Your Freedom Number shouldn't just be a "break-even" point, which doesn't give you any margin for error. That's why to be Free for Life™ in our community, you have to hit your Freedom Number with your passive income and then an *additional* 20 percent safe harbor.

So how do you assess your Freedom Number?

With new members, we start by working to determine the Freedom Number with both the member and the member's spouse, as the individual's definition of a freedom lifestyle often has some variances—both partners must be able to see "what's in it for me." Then we do the same calculations I did when I was first confronted with Jenna's illness.

What is the couple's lifestyle burn rate—that is, *What does it take to generate the cash flow needed to pay all the personal bills?* To pay your overhead lifestyle – your food or daily expenses, mortgage, utilities, cars, travel, healthcare, education, insurance, personal debt repayment – you have an amount, so what is it? It's okay to approximate this number on the first pass, but specificity in all things allows us to really measure progress, and it is the realized progression to a desired outcome that keeps the ball rolling. This is the exact opposite of the traditional Wall Street financial retirement models that contain no viable milestones or markers—it's all an "accumulation game" with no specified end point. Frustrating, right?

After digging through their paperwork, couples come up with the amount. Then we gross it up for taxes, at today's tax rates, using a multiplier of about 1.3. That works for most states except higher tax states like New York, New Jersey, Connecticut, and California, for which we use a multiplier of about 1.5 to calculate taxes. (Your CPA could provide the exact multiplier for you if you ask).

Then we take the total from a monthly number grossed-up for taxes, to an annualized number. So, let's say $20,000 per month, which would be $240,000 per year, gross pre-tax.

Then I will use a very conservative number in Freedom Founders—10 percent—which may not be conservative out on the "street," but 10 percent return on investment on capital assets (in up markets, sideways markets, and down markets) is a very conservative number for us to be able to achieve.

Knowing we need $240,000, and can get a minimum targeted 10 percent annual return, we then extrapolate the asset total of $2.4 million needed to produce the $240,000 annual passive income. With a specific number in mind, we can then reverse engineer to determine what capital assets are needed and how to get them on the fastest track without overarching risk. In doing this we create our member's Freedom Blueprint™.

In this scenario, the $2.4 million of deployable capital becomes the basis for creating the couple's Freedom Number. Economic freedom is in reach!

More than "Retirement" Assets

What's the common denominator among all the business owners I talk to? A lack of freedom. Chained to the business. The income is good and the lifestyle perks are great, but the price being paid is not a balanced trade for most of us. The question becomes, *Why do we go down such a path?* Answer: It's what we've been told. We bought into the propaganda, handed down from generation to generation, from parents and teachers, that education is the driver for higher income.

If a higher-income begets an elevated lifestyle dependent on the producer (you) to have to work harder, longer, and faster (more efficiency), where is the freedom you so greatly sought when you were putting in the time and money for the education? Perhaps you only received part of the education you needed. Who teaches "freedom" anyway?

No matter how much income you make from your career or business, do you ever have any certainty? Or do you constantly struggle to know when enough is enough?

After calculating my own Freedom Number, I soon saw a great need to do the same for others. At conferences with practice owners and in mastermind groups with business owners, I started sharing what I'd figured out, finding others eager to learn and do the same.

Most every business owner I spoke with was frustrated by the traditional approach to work, money, and retirement.

"Retirement" is an outdated construct. Today we are better able to maintain our health than in generations past, allowing us to live longer than our forebears and continue in business or active income if we wish. That means that age 80 is the new 65.

"Retirement" is an outdated construct.

Retirement-focused assets are equally outmoded. Whether it's a 401(k), stocks, bonds, annuities, mutual funds—or any financial products of that nature—does it make sense to tie up your money for decades on Wall Street, allowing others to control your money as a proxy without any certain criteria for success?

No matter which firm you work with or what product you buy, Wall Street's advice is typically the same: buy it, hold it, and let it grow for decades. In the meantime, because of the market's volatility, don't touch it. And try not to worry. Then, after spending half your life putting in as much as you can, enter "retirement," where you put your money in "safe investments" such as CDs, annuities, bonds, or T-Bills. The problem there is the return on safe investments is barely 1-2 percent—not enough to produce the cash flow needed. In addition, inflation or the cost of living will likely cause you to run out of investment assets far before your last days. For all its ingenuity, Wall Street has never created a viable plan that solves this problem.

Should an economic downturn hit your Wall Street investments in your later years, there is not time to make up the losses caused by stock market volatility. You can wipe out 30 percent of your assets and still survive when you're middle-aged, during your peak earning years. But you'll be hard hit if you're 75 and the market bottoms out!

I know story after story of those who retired right before the next market correction and found themselves in this very predicament. One day they feel pretty good about their financial future, and then along comes the dot-com tech bust of 2000 or the Great Recession of 2008 and it's "Hi-ho, hi-ho, off to work I go," facing the dread of being back in the workforce with neck and back pain and the vision of travel and leisurely mornings snatched away. Imagine Lucy snatching the football away from an on-rushing Charlie Brown, and you can picture what Wall Street's volatility has done to so many forlorn retirees.

During your earning years, if you're a relatively high-income business earner, a Wall Street advisor will likely recommend you to save anywhere from $5 million to $10 million over the course of your active career to be able to retire at the same lifestyle. For most of us, those numbers are out of reach!

The worst part? You'll spend decades trying to fork over $5 million or more to Wall Street, and never feel like you have enough. Even though you're working hard, running a respected business, providing for your family, and spending as much time cherishing what you love as you can, you'll still question your security *and* your freedom.

The worst part? You'll spend decades trying to fork over $5 million or more to Wall Street, and never feel like you have enough.

I've spoken with so many couples who despite working for 30 years still have their Wall Street advisor say, "You're a long way off before you can even *begin* to think about slowing down."

There's a better way.

It starts by discarding Wall Street's outdated "accumulation number." Because it doesn't matter how much you accumulate on Wall Street, or how much you put into savings—which in many ways is the same thing.

What truly matters is how you get your savings, your accumulated money, your hard-earned *capital*, working for you. *This* is the key to your freedom.

The Sustainability of Real Estate

In calculating my Freedom Number, the big question I asked was, "Did I have enough from *real estate* to provide cash flow on a sustainable, predictable basis?

While I could make money as a dentist, that money was active income, always dependent upon me trading hours for dollars, which isn't the same as wealth. Wealth is owning tangible assets—whether it's a business or real estate—that produce regular income because you're renting the asset out or providing services or products to somebody else who wants to use them.

Once more of a side pursuit and curiosity, real estate suddenly became my game plan.

It all started back in dental school when I realized real estate was an asset that gave me more control than any investment in the stock market. But exercising that control also took some time and effort. It wasn't really passive for me in the beginning. Over time, I learned better ways of achieving the capital base I wanted or needed in order to achieve and surpass my Freedom Number.

I learned how real estate can provide sustainable cash flow from people who mentored me in real estate and finance. These mentors practiced what they preached, and I wanted to be like them. They showed me how real estate gave them more control, cash flow, and time flexibility than anything found on Wall Street—once acquired and managed effectively and efficiently.

It took about a decade for me to learn and accumulate efficient skills in real estate, which I did while full-time as a business owner-operator of my dental practice. I enjoyed the pursuit, but I never considered leaving dentistry.

That changed with Jenna's recovery from her transplant when I realized real estate gave me the ability to sell the practice and spend more time with her. On top of that, real estate had given me so much more, including the skill sets to continue to build income; adaptability as I created more cash-flow producing assets; and flexibility, allowing me to transition from full-time active work to part-time.

Had I not invested in real estate, and instead chosen to invest my money with someone on Wall Street, I would've never developed the skills and experience real estate afforded me, which ultimately helped me orchestrate and own my freedom.

While there are plenty of technical, do-it-yourself books about real estate, I wrote this book to fill a gap in the literature for those who want the freedom that real estate provides without having to take on a second job or business. These readers are the high-income earners who I enjoy helping through the Freedom Founders community. They want to be their own financial advocate without the time and painful experience of becoming what I call "the accidental landlord." It's more important to understand the "what" and the "who" than the "how." Freedom Founders provides the "how" and, in so doing, collapses the time that it takes for our members to reach their Freedom Number.

Real estate taught me the five principles I describe in this book:

* ★ **Your Freedom Number**—how to know how much is enough, so you can choose freedom over uncertainty.
* ★ **The Power of Association**—how others will get you on the fast track to owning your freedom.
* ★ **Wealth Is What You Own, Not What You Do**—how real estate provides freedom with passive cash flow (as opposed to transactional income).
* ★ **Principles Before Strategies, Strategies Before Tactics**— how the definition of one's freedom provides the framework for the initiatives and the specific steps.
* ★ **Invest in Your Transferable Skill Sets**—how skills like marketing, sales, negotiation, leadership, and delegation will provide you sustainability in a fast-changing and volatile market economy.

Your Cash Flow Number

Your "cash flow" number is a much better target than an accumulation number.

When we talk about a cash flow number, it's not a guess. We don't suggest a range of "$5 million to $10 million," as Wall Street might push, because of the market's unknown future volatility.

Instead, we nail down a specific cash flow lifestyle number (aka Freedom Number), which allows us to target the specific capital investment amount deployed into capital assets that will produce the desired annuity cash-flow income. Like $2.4 million in deployable capital that can generate 10 percent annual interest to produce the $240,000 annual revenue. That's specific.

If you've worked fifteen years and thus far have $1.2 million in deployable capital—half of the $2.4 million you need—then you may think "I need to work another 15 years." But that's not the case if you understand how to orchestrate the growth of that capital (instead of saving or accumulating).

One of the benefits of investing in capital assets (real businesses, equipment, or my favorite, real estate) is the use of financial leverage. While many protest against the use of debt (because of "safety," "risk," and a model that "used to work"), the proper use of another person's or institution's money is the fastest way to grow capital assets. Real estate, in particular, has always been relatively easy to finance by banks. Why? Because of the stability of real estate throughout history, even during volatile market cycles. Ever try going to the bank and asking for a loan against your stock portfolio or your crypto account?

The use of financing to acquire and control capital assets allows for a force multiplier. The investor's cash-flow return on his actual cash investment is enhanced as are the tax benefits (another benefit of tangible assets) plus the growth or equity component.

Instead of working fifteen years longer to generate another $1.2 million in savings or 401(k) contributions, the use of financial leverage in aggregating real estate equities will increase the speed at which the Freedom Number is reached. Remember, the entire premise is that the metric that matters is *passive cash flow*—not accumulation. By focusing on the cash flow, the dollar amount of assets to create that cash flow is far less than the guidance provided by most financial advisors. This is the shift that literally changes the lives of those who learn to implement it. All fear and uncertainty are removed.

To understand the power of leverage, let's compare the two strategies. Suppose a single-family home rental is purchased for $100,000 and rented out for $1,200 per month or $14,400 a year. Of course, it's not all profit. An investor must account for operating expenses, including repairs, maintenance, insurance, and property taxes. The amount remaining after expenses is referred to as the Net Operating Income, or "NOI." In this example, the annual NOI is $8,640 for this single rental ($14,400 X 60 percent).

By utilizing leverage, the same $100,000 can purchase five $100,000 homes with 20 percent down ($20,000 X 5) while securing a 30-year mortgage for the remaining 80 percent. After subtracting operating expenses *and debt service*, the NOI results in $3,312 per year per house or a total of *$16,560* for the five homes. This is almost a 100 percent increase in cash flow utilizing the same $100,000, and we haven't even considered appreciation, amortization, or depreciation offsets!

No Leverage			
$100K	+ −		$100K Cash Purchase $1,200 / Mo Rental Income 40% Operational Expenses
💲	=		**$8,640 / Yr.** N.O.I.

Leveraged			
$20K	− + − −		$20K Down per Home $80K Finance per Home @5.3% $1,200 / Mo Rental Income per Home 40% Operational Expenses $444 Debt Service per Home
$20K			
$20K	=		$3,312 / Yr. N.O.I. per Home
$20K			
$20K	X		5 Homes
💲💲	=		**$16,560 / Yr.** N.O.I.

One word about inflation:

It's a growing concern, especially because it's been relatively low for the last several decades—but it won't stay that way forever. Most forecasts show inflation hiking up in the 2020s. Inflation works just like compound interest but in reverse. A 3 percent inflation factor will decrease the purchasing power of $100 today to only $74 in purchasing power in 10 years, a loss of 26 percent. A 5 percent inflation factor would reduce that same $100 to only $61 worth of goods or services in 10 years, a loss of 39 percent.

When you have a business, you can increase your revenue stream by increasing your prices. That's inflation, right? But when you're no longer working and living on a fixed income, there's no ratcheting up your prices. In Wall Street's accumulation model, you have to live off of what you've got (your nest egg is finite on Wall Street). That may mean you deplete your assets in addition to living off the interest income. Over time, your assets disappear completely.

Real estate, on the other hand, is a tangible asset that keeps pace with inflation both in the cash flow revenue and the value (equity) of the asset. You don't have to worry about depletion (having to sell your real estate for cash) in order to make up for the loss of purchasing power. The rent (which is the dividend that real estate provides with great stability and sustainability) will rise with the cost of living, thus protecting your ability to maintain your own lifestyle. Wall Street can't make that promise.

To learn more about real estate and its success during inflationary times I've created a free webclass for readers of *Own Your Freedom*. Visit www.OwnYourFreedomBook.com/Resources to access it for free.

A fairly well-known financial principal, the "Trinity Study," maintained that a Wall Street retirement account investment principal could be depleted or drawn down by 4 percent per year to provide monthly cash for up to 25 years. After 25 years, you'd be down to zero. Does anybody really want to plan like that? Does it make sense to put a ticking clock on the final third of your (and your spouse's) life? (Note: More recently, a large number of financial planners have reduced the depletion percentage down to 2.8 percent per year. You should ask yourself, "Why, what's changed?" Apparently, clients have been running out of money before running out of life under the 4 percent rule!)

A recent new member of the Freedom Founders community had this very same explanation given to him by his RIA (Registered Investment Advisor). After receiving this roadmap of his financial future, he decided it wasn't a goal he could live with. He and his wife found the alternative path provided by the Freedom Founders Blueprint gave them the certainty they wanted and, frankly, felt that they deserved.

Such is the misguided conventional wisdom most of Wall Street is holding onto. The "accumulation number" and the "4 percent rule"—these metrics aren't your Freedom Number. Same with the notion that: "Contributing to a 401(k) or investing in index funds will get me to my desired goal." Following the majority will get you average results. If that's all you want, then follow the crowd. If not, then isn't it time you considered a different path? Who cares about your money and your future more than you do? Yet the majority still abdicates their future to outside advisors who have themselves not reached true freedom. It's a safety-in-numbers phenomenon.

It's a relief for our members to hear they don't need $6 million, $8 million, or $10 million in accumulated investments—that the solution is an asset base of far less, orchestrated to produce a sustainable passive revenue stream that pays for your lifestyle—your Freedom Number. You don't have to worry about giving your money to Wall Street with a hope and a prayer as you wait to see how it turns out in 30 years.

Shoot for a Target: What Will You Do When You Hit It?

What's your "retirement" plan? Just work as hard as you can as long as you can? That's not a plan that will earn you freedom. Instead, use your Freedom Number like a target.

When you have a specific target, like a bullseye, then it's a lot easier to hit. A target gives you options. You can hit it and keep working as you were—or you can hit it and be confident you can move on to your "next." (See: My book, *What's Your Next?: The Blueprint for Creating Your Freedom Lifestyle.*)

That's better than the alternative. When many couples talk about retirement, it goes something like this: "I'm sixty-two. We've done quite well. Our kids are grown and we got them through school. But I'm fearful that if we stop now, we're stopping too soon. So we better stay at this for a few more years."

"Well, how many more years?"

"I guess I should probably do it until my back hurts or my neck hurts so much that I just can't do it anymore."

Once we have a target to shoot for—your Freedom Number—then a world of possibility opens up. When our Freedom Founders couples have a specific asset target based on their Freedom Number, everything changes. No longer do they live in frustration and desperation. There is a plan with an end point. It changes their demeanor because now they know there's *life* at the end of the tunnel.

> # It changes their demeanor because now they know there's *life* at the end of the tunnel.

Now there's a goal to shoot for, and it's not just some "out there" number that somebody made up—cross your fingers, hope for the best. It's an achievable number that defines your freedom point.

When you target a specific number, you see a pathway. From that pathway, we reduce the risk. We reduce the volatility of intangible assets. As our blueprint is based on tangible assets (real estate), we don't have to live with the emotional highs and lows that you typically experience on Wall Street.

Once the couple has the blueprint, our members start thinking about the possibilities—*What will I do when I hit my Freedom Number? How will I act? Where will I invest my time?*

You don't want to think you have to wait until some magical mystical someday called "retirement" when you can finally go sell the business and stop working. Do you really want to wait until that point in time, whether it's 60, 65, 70, or 75 before you actually start enjoying your freedoms? No, of course not.

You want to build joy in as many freedoms as you can as you're going along.

In late 2020 around Christmastime, I heard the story of a business owner and family man, 56 years old, who had a heart attack. According to colleagues, he coupled a never-say-never work ethic with the stress of running a business during the pandemic. It's unfortunate, but too often a reality. The stress of working for an unknown number is the greatest cause of relationship disharmony. And it doesn't have to be that way.

We all know stories of life or health ending "too soon," way before someone's time. Having a target relieves some of the stress that can otherwise be debilitating and allows for enjoying life now instead of waiting until we feel secure—a feeling that evades most until the end.

Worksheet Tools

In calculating your Freedom Number and blueprint to become Free for Life™, we use simple worksheets designed to best show you where you are, where you're going, and "the gap" in between. These include a capital organizer and "My Freedom Sheet."

Capital Organizer

This one-page sheet accounts for all your assets and "deployable capital." In Freedom Founders, for a prospective member to qualify, they must have $1 million or more of deployable capital or equity. Many hear this number and believe it means "cash in the bank," but we mean overall equity. The capital organizer clarifies our starting asset position and helps identify hidden assets such as "dead equity" or under-deployed equity that can be redeployed as working capital to move the needle closer to the Freedom Number. For example, I often find a member who has equity in a commercial office building. While it feels great to have an asset that is free and clear of debt, the equity is "dead." Equity of $500,000 working at 10 percent will produce $50,000 of annuity income per year or over $4,000 per month. If you haven't reached your Freedom Number, the capital organizer helps us discover minor strategic opportunities like these that propel you to freedom.

FREEDOM FRAMEWORKS

CAPITAL ORGANIZER

My Current Assets

Retirement Investment Accounts

401k . . . . $

IRAs *(Traditional, Roth, Self Directed)* . . . . $

Health Savings Account . . . . $

Coverdell or 529 Plan *(Education)*. . . . . $

Defined Benefit Plan . . . . $

Cash Balance Plan . . . . $

Other *(Precious Metals, etc.)*. . . . . $

Non-Retirement Financial Investments
(Stocks, bonds, mutual funds, annuities, REITs, cash-value life insurance)

#1 . . . . $

#2 . . . . $

#3 . . . . $

Cash Assets *(Cash or highly liquid assets)*

CD *(6 months or less maturity)*. . . . . $

Money Market Account . . . . $

Checking/Savings/Physical Cash . . . . $

Investment Real Estate Equity (Equity = current market value, minus loans)
(Equity of rental properties, commercial real estate, office building, etc.)

#1 . . . . $

#2 . . . . $

Other Under-Utilized Real Estate Equity

Equity in primary residence . . . . $

Additional residences (vacation homes, etc.). . . . . $

Lifestyle Equity *(Boats, luxury cars, etc.)*

#1 . . . . $

#2 . . . . $

Practice Valuation *(Only include if you desire to exit practice in the next 3-5 years)*

Approximate valuation of your primary practice . . . . $

Valuation of additional practices (if applicable). . . . . $

My Potential Investing Capital $

FREEDOM BLUEPRINT

MY FREEDOM SHEET

The FIVE Freedoms: *(Financial, Relationships, Time, Purpose, Health)*

....

....

....

....

I CONSIDER MYSELF FREE WHEN: ....

....

....

I DESIRE FREEDOM BECAUSE: ....

....

....

My Freedom Number

$ [____]	X	12	=	$ [____]	X	1.33	=	$ [____]
Monthly Lifestyle Income*				Annual Income		Taxes (25% gross increase)		**ANNUAL INCOME REQUIRED FOR FREEDOM**

		=	- $ [____]
[____]	Annual Income [____]		**ANNUAL PASSIVE INCOME**
Monthly Passive Income	Annual Income		

= $ [____]

GAP TO FREEDOM

*Monthly Lifestyle Income = The amount needed to cover monthly lifestyle expenses. DO include current personal debt obligation and debt amortization. DO NOT included expenses you run through your business

Closing the Gap - My Choices

WAYS TO DECREASE MONTHLY EXPENSES (BURN RATE) ....

....

....

....

WAYS TO INCREASE MONTHLY PASSIVE INCOME ....

....

....

....

Reverse Engineer

$100,000 ANNUAL PASSIVE INCOME REQUIRES:

Rate of Return	Capital Investment
@ 1%	$10,000,000
@ 5%	$2,000,000
@ 8%	$1,250,000
@ 10%	$1,000,000
@ 12%	$833,333

One of our mantras at Freedom Founders is: "You're closer than you think to owning your freedom."

One of our mantras is: "You're closer than you think to owning your freedom."

Oftentimes, for our new members, they become Free for Life™ within one to three years. These are the same people who had a Wall Street advisor who told them they needed to work a *decade longer* to put another couple million in the bank. Such a shift is life-changing!

Keep in mind, these members who become Free for Life™ in such a relatively short time aren't joining as babes in the woods. They aren't new graduates or young professionals. These are people who meet the criteria of $1 million or more in deployable capital. But even with that capital, it's finding their Freedom Number and creating the blueprint that helps them see how close they are.

Free for Life™ in three years? For our couples, that takes a huge load off their shoulders. Now they don't have to just "endure" their working future. Instead, they can look forward to *enjoying* the next three years and beyond.

Many couples experience a newfound sense of adventure. It's even more than *hope* because having a specific goal with a definitive blueprint in reach starts changing the way they think.

We have a plan and now we just have to work this plan.

And they don't have to work the plan alone. That's because we have both regular weekly Freedom Implementation Team (FIT) meetings with small groups and larger Freedom Founders member events. These help keep a pulse on progress, with guidance and accountability to get there.

The transformation of our people's lives is what provides the passion for what I do. It's my "reason why." It's my purpose.

Maslow's Hierarchy of Needs

Why is the Freedom Number the first principle?

In order to provide our essential needs—food, clothing, shelter, and the lifestyle and opportunities we want for our family—we need to capture those needs with a single metric: our Freedom Number.

As humans, we share the same set of needs. To eat, breathe, love, belong, and feel accomplishment.

Psychologist Abraham Maslow famously developed a hierarchy of needs, which posits that we have fundamental needs that must be taken care of first before we can take care of our other needs. For example, we must address our need for food and water before we pursue self-fulfillment.

The visual representation of Maslow's hierarchy is a pyramid, with the most basic physiological needs at the bottom and the most advanced, self-actualization, at the top.

When I look at this pyramid, I see the stages of my professional life. It's no surprise that when we're young, we're not focused on "significance and self-actualization." We're busy with school, launching a career, and starting a family. It's a lot. But at a certain point, we yearn for more freedom.

In Freedom Founders, our members are blessed that we've been able to sustain our needs for the first half of the pyramid. We've provided for our food, warmth, water, security, and safety, and feel a sense of belonging.

With those needs accounted for, our members are focused on the top half. These are things like deeper belonging, prestige, significance, and self-actualization—"the realization of one's full potential.[2]" For many, owning freedom presents the best opportunity for self-actualization.

Your Freedom Number Blueprint

To find your Freedom Number, we have a "blueprint day" in which we help you and your spouse create a blueprint. The blueprint creates your freedom plan outline based on your timeline, your definition of freedom, and the assets you already possess. It allows you to visualize who you are and what you've achieved so that you can best target your freedom goal.

The blueprint day provides a framework of clarity, outcome, and vision. To achieve clarity, we ask members to define freedom for themselves. *What does freedom really mean to you as a couple? Are you still working? Do you volunteer? What are you doing with your family? Friends? Do you travel? Where do you live? Do you still operate your business?*

2 "Maslow's hierarchy of needs," Wikipedia.org, accessed June 29, 2021, https://en.wikipedia.org/wiki/Maslow's_hierarchy_of_needs

Most people keep all this stuff in their heads rather than sharing it. Clarity remains elusive because it just rattles around in the noggin. Couples rarely talk about this stuff—it's hard to give voice to the things in life you have aspirations for but that aren't happening yet. It might make you feel like you're not achieving like "everybody else" in society, even though everybody else is having the same kinds of issues as you are. No one wants to admit what's behind their ego-driven image. But that doesn't solve the inner dilemma of a lack of freedom and no one to talk to—not even (especially) one's spouse. After all, we're supposed to be the protector of our family, right?

When you realize your freedom is something that can be defined, envisioned, and achieved, it opens the door to having those conversations with your spouse like you've never had before. There is almost instantaneous stress relief! At this point, the blueprint evolves.

I often hear during a blueprint day: "This is the first time we've ever been able to have these kinds of conversations." This is a game-changer!

The Freedom Blueprint itself is a powerful document because we create it in the present tense. To create the blueprint, we use a few solid tools (like the Capital Organizer and Personal Key Assessment) asking deep questions as we go.

For example, when calculating your Freedom Number, you'll want to account for your non-negotiables.

What would you not *sacrifice? What would you absolutely not give up in creating your Freedom Blueprint?*

Non-negotiables could include:

* ★ Time with family
* ★ Where you live
* ★ Not taking on any new debt

★ A cherished property, like a family farm or a vacation home

★ Acting in an unethical manner

The blueprint exercises help you make choices based on your definition of freedom, your values, and your capital base—not based on just emotions.

We close out this chapter with a snippet of the questionnaire, and some actual responses. You'll see these questions get the members thinking about their life in the future. We ask that they respond in the present tense—as if they're already doing what they envision they'll do in the future. For example, "In the future, when I own my freedom, I'm stress-free." You'll also see that the responses are focused on achieving the top half of Maslow's pyramid: love, belonging, significance, and self-actualization.

What's your definition of freedom?	"Retired self-exploration and continued learning."
How do you act?	"Will always want the best for others."
Do you do any active work?	"Yes, but on my terms."
What are you passionate about?	"Being able to teach my philosophy of life."
What gives meaning in your life?	"My children. My wife, a few friends. Recognition."
What are your non-negotiables?	"Quality time with family and serving in my church."
How do you act?	"Without stress or fear."
Do you do any active work?	"Farming and fixing up cars."
What are you passionate about?	"Building a legacy of quality more than financially."
What gives meaning in your life?	"Seeing my kids progress and helping others."
What challenges you?	"Helping other people and building teams."

We live our lives with so many questions and so few answers. The uncertainty can be exhausting. By asking the *right* questions about your future, you can find the best answers that'll help you determine your Freedom Number. This is where it starts.

But just knowing your Freedom Number isn't enough. It's just one of five principles, which you'll need to work on all at the same time (simultaneous, not sequential) to truly own your freedom.

GREG & JACKIE'S BLUEPRINT STORY

Greg and Jackie Linney came to their first Freedom Founders meeting about two years ago, after reading an article I had written in a dental publication. Greg is the dentist, Jackie is the office manager, and for the past thirty years, they've run a marvelous practice in Sugarland (near Houston), Texas. They love life, love to travel, have two grown kids, and enjoy a second home in Palm Springs, California.

They had reached a point where they considered selling the practice. On their blueprint day, they shared the big fear that everybody has: *Do I have enough?*

In creating their blueprint, we looked at their Freedom Number and their assets—such as stocks and bonds, 401(k), equity in the office building, equity in the business, and their homes.

Then with pen and paper, we started rearranging the equity investments, targeting growth and cash flow.

Once we assembled those pieces in place for Greg and Jackie, it became very apparent that they had enough if they redeployed what they had into cash-flowing real estate assets. They just needed to go forward. Greg and Jackie left the blueprint day with excitement and confidence.

Greg and Jackie moved quickly. Once they joined Freedom Founders, they deployed $1 million-plus capital within three months. Within that same period of time, they also started getting regular cash flow checks—the actual passive income that comes off the assets. This is what builds confidence quickly—when the actual revenue begins to flow (mailbox money!). They'd never experienced this before in their entire working life.

Once the checks started coming in, they were motivated to do even more, so they started the process of selling the practice. Close to the finish line, the deal with the buyer fell through. It was tough, and I could see it took a bit of wind out of their sails. Undeterred, they stuck with the plan, and nine months later sold the practice to another buyer. This transition was meant to be.

They love to travel. They love to play tennis. They love to hike. And they love to mentor younger people, which they started doing formally with Freedom Founders, as leaders of the FIT group for our new members.

Every quarter, Greg and Jackie mentor those coming on board as new Freedom Founders, because they're such strong leaders and they've been through the system. They understand the process, they bring confidence to the group, and they love doing it. It's a volunteer position, it's not paid, but they love to do it anyway because that's who they are.

Two years ago, Greg and Jackie were able to make a great transition with confidence because they had their Freedom Number in place. And now they are really owning their freedom every day.

View Greg and Jackie's full interview and the specific steps they took to freedom by visiting www.OwnYourFreedomBook.com/Resources. While you're there, watch my free webclass 'How Much Is Enough' to determine where you're at and where you want to go.

CHAPTER 3

THE EVOLUTION OF A FREE PERSON

BY DAN S. KENNEDY

You do NOT start out as a Free Person. Not even now, in America. Not even close.

> *Hi Ho, Hi Ho, It's Off To Work I Go,*
> *For I Have Bills To Pay Today*
> *For The Hamburgers I Ate Yesterday!*

Almost everybody starts "in chains," notably including the pressing and constant NEED to make a buck today to pay yesterday's light bill. This commands and controls, compelling all sorts of decisions, including NOT being selective, discriminating, or strategic about the kind of customers brought through the doors—the development of a business that you desire and will be thrilled to wake up living in every morning 3, 5, 7 years into the future. NEEDINESS of any kind *imprisons*. FEAR, anxiety, worry, uncertainty about "making enough" *controls*.

Next, if not careful, the professional owner conforms to "*the* plan of progress" his peers a decade or two ahead of him have followed, and industry leaders teach—only to one day realize they are working for (enslaved by) their practice, rather than the owner of a business that works for them. They say: "How the devil did THIS happen?"

About that time, many begin an arduous, difficult process of **_trying_** *to free themselves* from the financial prison of their business, their continuing NEED for earned income to pay lifestyle bills, and funding the suddenly near "retirement."

This all largely ignores and, to various degrees, conflicts with both The Evolution of a Free Person and, more importantly, THE BIG SECRET to accelerating that evolution. I'm excited about talking about both of these things with you in this chapter, and I'll tell you in advance that Dr. Phelps personally, successfully used THE ACCELERATION SECRET, so is therefore ideally qualified to help you do the same.

FROM DRAGGING YOUR KNUCKLES TO WALKING UPRIGHT – FINANCIALLY

It starts with being a Technician or Clinician, what I sometimes describe as being "a Doer of your Thing." A lot of people stop right there, and after 30, 40, even 50 years are still there, having wittingly or unwittingly become a captive of their single, narrowly focused skill-set. **From there, next, a person raises up and walks** *a little* **taller, as a Business/Practice** *Operator*.

He still devotes the majority of his time to being and always improving as a Doer of His Thing, but he also adds the running and managing of the business activities attached to it and necessary for it. He often thinks of these as "necessary evils," and musters little real interest or enthusiasm for them.

Next, third, he evolves in his mindset, thinking, and interests and becomes the Business *Owner*. Now he gets really "into" the business aspects. It's here that a lot of owners first sign up with management programs and join coaching groups.

Next, fourth, or "in concert with," he becomes a *Chief MARKETING Officer* of his business; what I call an upward promotion from Doer of Thing to MARKETER of Thing. Whether you like acknowledging it or not, the bigger money and monetary rewards are with the marketing.

Next, fifth, while continuing with some percentage of attention and time in all roles, he stands fully upright as *Entrepreneur*. This is really the start of liberation; using a broader knowledge base and skill-set to expand the core business and often diversify, creating multiple income streams.

Finally, sixth, *Investor*. Still, also, most or all of the other roles, but evolving to Investor. As an Investor, he thinks (very) differently about his own practice and the requirements that it be a great investment he would gladly make each day and that it pays him yield and appreciation. He creates more liberation by making money make money for him, notably, passive income, not just active, earned income from his or his team's work. This sixth step in The Evolution of a Free Person is the biggest step of them all. The most *sophisticated* step.

IT IS (ONLY) THE 5TH AND 6TH STEPS THAT GET YOU TO A VITALLY IMPORTANT OBJECTIVE: EQUITY VS. INCOME.

Fundamentally, you are wealthy (and financially independent and secure) by what you OWN, not by what you earn. Earned income, by its nature, gets spent. It pulls off an amazing magic act: it disappears! Many, even after raising their income year over year after year, sit at the kitchen table once a year and ask aloud: "Where DID all that money go?"

Personally, I vividly remember once thinking that making a million dollars a year was the same as being a millionaire, and the top of the mountain, the be-all 'n end-all. Imagine my ultimate disappointment! I (stupidly) spent about 10 years as a *HIUI* – High Income, Under-Invested – before I "got right" with Money. Evolved to thinking about *everything* as an Investor. Made creating EQUITY the priority over just making Income. Measuring, "live time," my progress with Equity, not just counting Income. I evolved this into a strategy I call PRESENT BANK/FUTURE BANK, and the importance of NOT making daily deposits only to the PRESENT BANK ACCOUNT.

Of course, you *can* argue that you are "automatically" building up (captive) equity in your business or practice, and that is so, although it is waiting to pay you until the Someday of its sale. For example, many doctors are unpleasantly surprised at the *actual* equity there's a buyer available for, the amount of (risky) owner financing needed, and/or the extended enslavement to the Corporate or Private Equity buyer – for 2, 3, or 5 years that seem like an eternity. Some are also surprised by the big, lump-sum tax consequences. In recent years, the yield on savings and conservative investments (the kind you make when you've disconnected the replacement income spigot) has been so low as to force holding onto the practice and moving the Someday goal-posts, again, and again. In simple terms, this single-source, captive equity isn't all it's cracked up to be!

The far better "plan" utilizes…

THE ACCELERATION SECRET
to Escape From Financial Prison

Here it is: make a BIG note: "SIMULTANEOUS, *NOT* SEQUENTIAL."

We are conditioned from childhood forward to think and act sequentially. First grade first, second grade second. Scouts, athletics, military service, etc. – climbing ladders one rung at a time. It's important to understand that this is as much a means of controlling populations as it is anything else. The way this extends into your relationship with money is *not* necessarily helpful. At best, it lays out a slow path. First, establishing and growing one's income until there is enough *extra* money to start saving. Next, second, starting to invest only after there is enough *extra* income *and* enough accumulated in savings to make investing "worth doing." Next, third, moving from haphazard investing to "plans," typically provided by others, like *automatic* contributions to 401K or similar retirement accounts, automatic accumulation of equity in your home, maybe your practice's office building. It should be obvious that this can be a long, slow journey, with a number of opportunities to stall out along the way. A lot of people never make it from start to finish, or if they do, it takes so long that the fruits of it all aren't very sweet. You see this illustrated, for example, on cruises, populated by aged people who have waited and saved and waited some more to finally start crossing items off of a bucket list. There they are, barely able to navigate the buffets, on their walkers!

THE ACCELERATION SECRET is to scrap the "board game" set-up and step away from your conditioned sequential thinking and, instead, in its place, think and act simultaneously on every one of the steps. This is a significant "secret" to Dr. Phelps's success at achieving financial freedom early, not late, and in a relatively short number of years. He began investing nearly at the same time he began earning. His story always reminds me of Arnold Schwarzenegger's wealth secret. Having immigrated here with nominal resources, starting a climb to fame as a competitive bodybuilder while also supporting himself doing landscaping, bricklaying, and other similar work, then moving to acting, literally from Day One of earning, he simultaneously began saving and quickly investing. He was using a large portion of his income for down-payments on real estate investments before he even had his own rented apartment let alone a house; while he was camping out on friends' coaches, a few weeks or months here, a few weeks or months there. He thought and acted simultaneously, not sequentially.

HE BEGAN INVESTING NEARLY AT THE SAME TIME HE BEGAN EARNING.

Your immediate temptation may be to say "Well, they did this when young. It's too late for me to start this." Jeff Bezos, founder and still leader of Amazon, says their mandate is to treat every day as a new Day One. And, if you are able and willing to "model" someone or some others who have used Simultaneous, Not Sequential, you can shorten the number of years required to achieve a particular result – such as establishing passive income equal to, as replacement of your active earned income – by a lot. Dr. Phelps has codified his experience with this into a system any professional can use, in just a three to seven-year time frame.

YOU CAN TRIGGER
"THE PHENOMENON®"
IN YOUR LIFE – NOW, ON PURPOSE

The Phenomenon® is **the unique time in a person's life when they accomplish more in 10 months than they did in the prior 10 years!** This happens. Often. In fact, most celebrities, entrepreneurs, CEOs, athletes, politicians, and others you know of, who are famous as successes, have a Phenomenon® period in their life stories. They may or may not talk about it. You may or may not know of it. But if you dig, you will, 9 out of 10 times, find it.

I have been very fortunate to experience The Phenomenon® not just once but several specific times. When I say "very fortunate" I mean it, and I mean it as an expression of gratitude. However, I'll also take credit for a good-sized share of that being fortunate thing!

Many people experience their Phenomenon® serendipitously, produced by a convergence of actions, activities, made connections, and even "good fortune." If you carefully dissect and analyze their seemingly sudden leap from being an unknown to fame, from poverty to riches, from running in place, stuck, to racing forward, you will unearth a shortlist of shared-in-common "triggers" of their "Phenomenons®."

Armed with these, you can act intentionally and deliberately to "trigger" your Phenomenon®, rather than waiting for it to occur organically. YOU can intentionally and deliberately trigger YOUR Phenomenon®, now, not later.

There are six principal Triggers:

★ Decision

★ (Re-Allocated) Investment (of Attention & Money)

★ Viable Opportunities

★ Productive Association(s)

★ Action, Action, Action!

★ (Cautiously) Saying YES More Often Than NO

DECISION IGNITES

You decide – to do different things AND to do things differently, in the acquisition of know-how, expansion of skill-set, connection to useful people, groups, and opportunities, ultimately RE-ORGANIZING the way you approach your financial freedom "north star" as well as other goals. Your decision is what ignites everything. You decide What (specific goals), Why (the motivation for them), When (the timeline and benchmarks), How (new actions), and Who (can help).

The vital word in all this is YOU. Forget whatever decisions have been sold to you, made for you, seem to be pre-destined. No one else and no circumstances have any right to your decisions.

RE-ALLOCATED ATTENTION
Of Time & Money

Napoleon Hill, author of *Think and Grow Rich* and *Laws of Success,* both from the late 1930s, wrote about something he called "sex transmutation" as an explanation for so many men not "hitting their stride" in business and financial successes until they passed age 40, often age 50. Hill said that until then so much of their attention was allocated to the pursuit of sexual partners and romantic activity it, as he put it, which too often drained the batteries and consumed vital resources. It's an interesting theory, isn't it? We might also **think of early years as having so much attention allocated to earning that establishing wealth and financial freedom is neglected. Certainly, whatever you focus your attention on tends to crowd out many other things.**

When you re-allocate your attention, time, and financial resources to developed, specific financial freedom objectives, you "automatically" alter what you even notice and take note of, hear and overhear, think about, converse about, and attract into your life. *Focus precedes achievement.*

In practical application, this means making a close, detailed examination of what consumes your time, energy, attention, and money passing through your hands now. Then you can make decisions about re-allocation. To offer an over-simplified example, the couple taking 3 vacations a year might agree to cut back to 1 a year for the next 5 years, to re-allocate the money spent on the other 2 to buying a rental property each year instead. The doctor putting in clinical time 9:00 – 5:00, 5 days a week might tighten that schedule, impose more qualifying restrictions on new patients accepted, to liberate 1 day a week for "studying up" on financial matters, using a "curriculum" of his devising, including taking somebody he is confident is financially freer than he is to lunch[3], reading a selection of books, taking web-based

---

3 "Take A Millionaire To Lunch" comes from one of the legendary success authors, lecturers, and teachers, Jim Rohn. Jim talked about advising poor people to find millionaires to take to lunch (to ask them questions and pick their brains). Jim said he almost always heard outrage: "Hey, why should I take some millionaire to lunch? He can afford to buy my lunch but I certainly can't afford to buy his!" This misses the point – which is the point! Jim meant it as both actual advice and as euphemism for the practice of seeking out and investing in know-how you lack but need to achieve your goals.

classes, joining an investor group and attending its meetings. In concert with this, I recommend a tactic called "Time-Blocking," one in a portfolio of assertive self-management and time management tactics in my book *No B.S. Time Management for Entrepreneurs (Third Edition)*.

VIABLE OPPORTUNITIES

THE PHENOMENON® **can't occur inside too small of a box.** Your mind must be opened to a wider range of options and opportunities for achieving your goals than it has been, otherwise you are guilty of the classic definition of insanity: doing the same things the same way but hoping for different results.

Care must be taken *not* to randomly, wildly "chase financial rabbits" that you know little or nothing about. You must be STRATEGICALLY open to more diverse opportunities, or at least to a second opportunity beyond the earned income of a practice. Most professionals (doctors, lawyers, etc.) are well-advised to find trustworthy, expert guides to assist with this.

As something of an aside, you ideally want an opportunity that does not merely replicate the same situation you are already in with your business – trading hours for dollars, having to actively produce all the gains. You want an opportunity that counter-balances the weaknesses of your small business with its specific strengths. It's on this basis, when asked, that I advise business and private practice owners against MLM/network marketing business opportunities and day-trading of stocks or options. I have nothing against either, when right for a person, at the right time in their life. But they are fragile by nature and demand a great deal of active labor and time taken away from the principal, certain income producer, the business.

PRODUCTIVE ASSOCIATIONS

We have given this a lot of comment elsewhere in this book, so I won't long belabor the point. Suffice to say that, to the extent you replace attention, interest, and time spent with unconstructive, unproductive associations with deliberately chosen and developed constructive, productive associations relevant to your stated goals, you increase the likelihood of The Phenomenon® being triggered. This is a simple, even obvious *equation,* yet few people use it to manage their affairs. I can assure you that exceptionally successful people do, in fact, use it.

ACTION, ACTION, ACTION!

My friend, famous author Robert Ringer's motto about this is: "*nothing* happens until *something* moves." Another long-time friend and colleague, the late Gary Halbert – so famous as a marketing "genius" he was the only such person to be remarked on by Johnny Carson, featured in The National Enquirer, and used in a Jeopardy answer – constantly asserted that "motion beats meditation." Dr. Maxwell Maltz, author of one of the all-time bestselling success books, Psycho-Cybernetics, with whom I co-wrote an up-date, The New Psycho-Cybernetics, said that motion was a better choice than delay or procrastination, because "course correction" toward a goal was only possible if moving. General Norman Schwarzkopf, famous for leading "Desert Storm," a speaking colleague on 20-plus events a year for several years, seconded that same idea, saying he'd rather be navigating and commanding changes in movement than trying to get a dead-stopped train going. You will find some version of the same fundamental concept stated in the interviews and autobiographies or biographies of virtually EVERY hyper-successful inventor, innovator, entrepreneur, investor, and goal achiever – from a Steve Jobs back to Walt Disney to top tier investors like Buffet, Rogers, and Zell.

I have long adhered to a personal practice of taking *some* start-up action for every idea, immediately upon getting and having interest in it, to begin assessing its viability by the "reaction of reality," rather than just consideration of it. This is to avoid a good idea "dying on the vine," a good opportunity being suffocated.

My father often counseled that "the road to hell is littered with good intentions." **Bluntly, good intentions are no better than no intentions at all if not fed and fueled by action.**

Sometimes the first actions can be "information assembly," from varied sources including networks and mastermind groups you belong to, trusted coaches or advisors you rely on, and accessed resources in media. You can never know everything; you'll be stalled and stuck forever, but knowing what you can know within a reasonable period of time is sensible. Still, some deadline must be set for a decision and then either a collection of actions or the abandonment of the intention altogether, so space exists for a different, more viable one.

(CAUTIOUSLY) SAYING YES MORE OFTEN THAN SAYING NO

The word in parentheses – CAUTIOUSLY – is an important one. All entrepreneurs and investors try to *manage* risks, *not take* risks. But they cannot and do not entirely avoid risks either. Buffet has said that a desire to never err, never get egg on your face, is far too crippling; you must strive to be right more often than not, and careful in proportion to the risks inherent in each particular decision. This describes a rational, measured approach.

A lot of "expert advisors" like lawyers and CPAs are quick to recommend you say NO to just about *everything*. THEIR interests are most safely served that way; they incur less risk of being blamed for you NOT doing anything than by you doing something.

In THE HOBBIT, the character Bilbo Baggins decries "adventures" because they can make you late getting home for dinner. But carefully chosen "adventures" are an important trigger for The Phenomenon®. Saying YES to a new and different place, group of people, collection of thinking on a subject, to things as simple as foods or genre of literature or film, is the only way we can "bump up against" opportunities for growth or gain what would otherwise be hidden from us, even if existing just across town. I remember being literally dragged to a Thai restaurant for the first time and discovering, to my surprise, that I liked it. I am always surprised to encounter people who have never seen Hitchcock movies or read great mysteries, sometimes proud of themselves for not wasting their time on "fiction," unaware of the many things that can be learned and ideas inspired by others' storytelling. Survey data from the financial industry reveals a top reason that people essentially stay ignorant of all opportunities and investing strategies is FEAR – of being embarrassed, of "being sold something." In every such case, ALL adventure, i.e., venturing out to see what one might see, is precluded.

I am of an age when you can look backward and consider what has occurred by the times you said Yes to something and the times you said No to something; by the times you were courageous and the times you were stayed by fear. And I have packed a lot into my years, including two wives and three marriages, two complete geographic relocations, simultaneous participation in three professions – ultimately leading each field, starting, buying, growing, and selling companies, being a much-published author, owning Standardbred racehorses, and driving professionally in harness races for twenty years, managing My Business Of My Money, investing in real estate, stocks, notes, startups, collector automobiles, and rare books, and more. There are a lot of Yeses and a lot of Noes to look back on. My conclusion, emphatically, is that most of the Yeses turned out better than the No in the same situation would have. Some quickly, some over time after some difficulty. Many of the Noes now seem prescient and wise and "whew, dodged a bullet on that one," but close to as many now beg having said Yes instead. There is a line in a Sinatra song: "…regrets? I have a few but then again, too few to mention." Were I to list mine, they would be more comprised of Noes that I now wish I'd said Yes to, than of anything else.

You Can MAGNETIZE YOURSELF, To The Phenomenon®

There is an unusual "magnetic effect" you will experience, as you get very clear on your major goals and develop what Hill called "definiteness of purpose" about your financial freedom: opportunities for new, relevant, and helpful associations; profitable investment; and other advancement toward those goals **WILL "APPEAR."** Some will have been "around" but not noticed by you until you made yourself magnetic to them. This is somewhat like buying a particular new car you hadn't seen on the roads much but after buying yours you suddenly see a lot of other people driving the same model. Where were they? There all along, of course, but you were blind to them because you were not attuned to them. Others that APPEAR will come from previously unknown or surprising sources and may involve people, places, or things you would previously have ignored or ruled out instantly and automatically that you should now say some sort of cautious Yes to. Or at least: Maybe.

There is a thing called a SCOTOMA. It's a medical term you probably know, loosely translated as having a "blind spot." A blockage to seeing certain things or in certain directions. You can have an intellectual or emotional scotoma. A firmly set blind spot toward certain opportunities or strategies and pathways forward. This creates *automatic* No's, and they bear just as much potential harm as do uninformed, impulsive Yeses. When you deliberately quell these automatic No's and make yourself open to thoughtful investigation and consideration of whatever is magnetically attracted to you by your clarity of purpose, you open the door to the unexpected but most welcome Phenomenon®.

There you have them: the most consistent triggers of The Phenomenon®, that time when you accomplish more tied to your chief goals in 10 months than in the previous 10 years. If you were stuck, you get un-stuck. If you saw only one narrow path, you discover choices of roads to desired destinations. If the goalposts of financial freedom kept getting pushed back, they'll stop running away – you'll suddenly advance down the field toward them with one big play after another. This is the experience in store for you, by these triggers.

CHAPTER 4

PRINCIPLE № 2:
THE POWER OF ASSOCIATION

BY DR. DAVID PHELPS

"You are the average of the five people
you spend the most time with."

Jim Rohn

hen we talk about "association," what do we mean? How is association more than just the people in your life? Do these people help you provide more freedom? Or more security? Or neither? In this chapter, we take a second look at those with whom we associate. There is wisdom all around us. Sometimes, we just need to get outside our comfort zone to find it. Look for advice from those who own their freedom.

OwnYourFreedomBook.com   83

FREEDOM QUESTIONS:

·····································

Do your associations contribute more to
your freedom or do they possibly hinder your
movement toward freedom? When meeting and
interacting with others, does your ego lead the
way? Do you feel you must ride higher than the
rest of the tribe? Who do you get guidance from?
How are they best qualified to guide you?

It was 2010, and the idea for what would become Freedom Founders was just starting to take shape. I had recently sold my practice for the second time. Cashed out, I no longer had the responsibilities of running a business. I was also realizing that for the first time in my life, I really had *freedom*. Freedom to invest time with my daughter, Jenna, unconstrained by the obligations of active income. Freedom to explore my frontiers and figure out what I want to do under my terms, not the terms of an industry or profession.

Sure, I could go back to dentistry, work for a day or two per week, if I wanted. But because I had achieved financial freedom, I had other options. And I couldn't get past a thought: *How can I give back and share some of my experiences and what I've learned in life to help others?*

So, as I was working through the fuzzy idea of what Freedom Founders could be, I attended a mastermind meeting.

In this small, intimate mastermind group, sitting around a table of five, also sat a young man in his late thirties, who did business coaching. I articulated to the group my aspirations, trying to get clarity. I mentioned how as a dentist I figured out how to get out of dentistry, how to run a better business, and some of the failures I had and lessons learned along the way. Then I also shared the other side of me: real estate, and how I had learned to create additional wealth and passive cash flow outside of dentistry.

"I don't see how the two sides of me fit together," I said. "I like real estate, but I don't see how my experience in dentistry and practice management fits with my knowledge of real estate investment. What do I do with these seemingly disparate components of my life, dentistry and real estate?" (What I didn't realize at the time is that limiting one's options to binary choices reflects a lack of creativity— exactly the reason I needed to be right where I was, in a mastermind group of my entrepreneurial peers.)

> ## What do I do with these seemingly disparate components of my life, dentistry and real estate?"

The young man at my table said, "Well, David, you don't really know exactly what's going to have traction, what's going to work, until you take some kind of action, some kind of step forward. Otherwise, you'll just keep spinning these ideas in your head. And you'll just keep wondering, *"Will this work? Will that work?"* without actually testing.

"So why don't you just call up a few of the people in your circle of influence – your friends, your colleagues – and just say, "Hey, come over to the house to the backyard. Let's have a little get-together. I want to explore some ideas with you. I'm not there to sell you anything.""

It was great advice. Before I had a vision of what Freedom Founders could be, I needed to do some exploring. I needed to bring together a group of people I could serve to test what I offered, talk about my story, and share how I figured out how to use real estate to grow out of dentistry and achieve freedom. I'd see what resonates, what they like or respond to, and get feedback. Only then would I have the clarity to take the next steps.

So I did that. Based on my colleague's advice, I took a small step forward. I had a casual session with a small group gathered at my home. That conversation is where the pearls of wisdom and the ideas that became Freedom Founders really started to flow. And from that I got a little bit more clarity on freedom itself. I discovered freedom was then and remains the common denominator of what business owners like me long to achieve. (Money is only a goal for the exchange of *time*—it's not the money we want in the end. It is freedom!)

For our next step, we rented a small meeting room at a hotel. I did a bigger invite and got about 25 people to come to a three-hour session. It was a bit more formalized, with me presenting from the front of the room some frameworks, components, and key questions I'd added from my backyard session.

From there, we grew Freedom Founders into what it is today: A formidable group of like-minded business entrepreneurs on a journey to freedom together. All because of a nudge from a friend during a mastermind group.

We don't get clarity on any potential initiative until we take a step forward. Until then, we live only with dreams of what "could be," fearing any change that might upset the status quo. And stepping forward largely results from the feedback and perspective we get in our associations with other people.

That's why we must think of our associations as an asset. The people in our circle, those who we spend our time with, are our *human capital*, also sometimes referred to as relationship capital. We invest in these people, and they return the investment in myriad ways.

We all have associations in our life. We start with our immediate family—those who raise us and who we grow up with. We have friends and colleagues, and likely feel belonging with a larger community.

But similar to how in earlier chapters we redefined the idea of *work*, here we need to redefine our *associations*.

In this chapter, we're not looking at our associations with cold, calculating eyes. We're not using relationships to dig for gold or to get a quid pro quo. Our definition of associations doesn't dehumanize the people in our life. Quite the opposite, in fact.

Instead, let's see the humans around us as who they are: humans. And humans value relationships. Humans benefit from relationships. Our associations help us grow.

Most of all, our associations can do one of two things: provide more security or contribute to more freedom. And some can do both! But beware of negative associations that may hinder your freedom objective.

In this way, association should be thought of as an asset that helps us *own our freedom*.

> ## In this way, association should be thought of as an asset that helps us *own our freedom*.

Your associations include:

* ★ Immediate family—some you may choose, some you don't.
* ★ Strategic associations or study clubs, which might be specifically to support your business.
* ★ Mentors and coaches.
* ★ Community service organizations like Rotary, Kiwanis, and Lions Club.
* ★ Business organizations or communities like Entrepreneur's Organization, Young Presidents' Organization, or Vistage.

> Freedom Founders is likewise a community association. Get a glimpse of what I mean by community and like-mindedness by going behind the scenes at one of our Freedom Founders events www.OwnYourFreedomBook.com/Resources.

Communities and associations have different meanings and purposes for each of us. The topic I cover in this chapter is how associations help us own our freedom.

The Power of Association

Jim Rohn—of the many quotes that he espoused over his lifetime—famously said, "You are the average of the five people you spend the most time with." He was speaking to this theme: to choose carefully the people with whom you associate.

This statement refers to research proving that our lives are heavily influenced by our relationships. Our connections influence our thinking, self-esteem, and decision-making.

My interpretation of this quote is simple: You don't want to be the smartest one in the room. Think about it. Wherever you go, if you're always the smartest person in the room, then you're learning nothing from anyone.

Instead, you really want to be in a group where you feel like, at best, you're an *equal*, with different skill sets and experiences than the others.

Look for groups where you're at the *lower* tier of experience or net worth, or business size—or whatever it is. You want to be in the lower tier so you can learn from others, allowing their wisdom to help you grow to their level.

In some groups, you may wish to elevate to a leadership role, providing mentoring for those who are newer. Teaching others what we have learned helps us embrace our philosophy and concepts of our experience and journey. It solidifies our own understanding of freedom principles.

Here's a quick story: When I was in eighth grade, growing up in Colorado, there was a YMCA bus on Saturdays that would take us up to the local ski resort.

That season, I'd ride up with Dixon, another kid in my same grade. Dixon was very athletic, one of those guys who could play every sport and do so at a pretty high level. The same with skiing. Dixon was definitely a better skier than I was. He was so good that there weren't any other skiers on the bus who could match him. So Dixon would often ski alone.

Well, it just so happened that one day, as we were taking the Saturday bus trip to the mountain, Dixon tapped me on the shoulder.

"Hey, David, want to ski together?"

I kind of gulped, because I knew this guy's a really good skier. But it worked out well, because as we know, if you're pushed beyond your comfort level, then you can increase your abilities.

That season, I became a much better skier, just because I started from a lower place and associated with someone who was at a much higher level. That's just one example of the power of association.

When you surround yourself with people whom you believe are wise and have more experiences, you can't help but learn something about yourself. Maybe they've gone down a path like yours, or their values in life are similar to what you believe too. Whatever it is, know that if you follow those kinds of people, they're going to help raise you up because that's what associations do.

Find People outside Your Comfort Zone

Most people don't go out of their way to find competitive people who can bring out the best in them. To find them, you must have the intention. You rarely find those people accidentally.

Just like my recommendation to participate in capitalism by owning assets, here I share why you must participate in your association to best ensure you own your freedom.

Just like my recommendation to participate in capitalism by owning assets, here I share why you must participate in your association to best ensure you own your freedom.

Why do so few of us go outside our comfort zone and step into rooms where everyone is smarter than us?

Early in life, we're put into groups. In school, we're placed with our peers. If we have academic prowess, perhaps we're grouped with others like us in the same class. Or perhaps we join a club or a team, and grow by competing with others.

During our school years, we have a mostly passive approach to association. We're not going out of our way to associate with a higher-tier peer group. We're just placed where we are and mostly live with it.

Even in college, most of us just take the requisite classes and spend time with groups that share our interests. Again, we're rarely taking an active approach to step into a room where everyone is smarter than us.

Then, once we're out of school, that's it! No more learning. Few of us choose to associate with people who challenge us. Pride and ego take over. We think we've reached the pinnacle of education and the path to success is now a given. What coaching or mentoring we had in our schooling suddenly disappears.

Perhaps in our work life, we face *some* challenges from higher tiers. Your peers, your boss—they get you to focus on your technical skills for greater productivity and efficiency. That said, typically these work associations are driving you to become a better *worker*—keeping you stuck in active income. Think about it. Everyone has their own agenda, and it doesn't include yours. You have to intentional in creating your own, otherwise other people will substitute their agenda for your freedom.

Seldom do we seek in our work life any associations who help us understand and nurture our own freedom.

That's why associations – groups, coaches, mentors, and more – must continue on some regular pace for us. We must strive to level up our associations, learning as much as we can from our peers, then learning more from our higher-ups.

I've been a member of lots of different groups over the years, and continue my association with many of those. But I didn't really appreciate my associations until later in my career. In fact, I was in my forties before I figured it out. Had I known or been exposed to the power of association when I was younger, I would have very likely elevated my own path to freedom even sooner!

That said, I did have one association early on that completely changed my life.

Because of my curiosity, from a young age, I started reading about finance and investing. I gravitated toward the real estate side (as opposed to the Wall Street side), in large part because of my understanding of the books I read. I followed through on the authors' recommendations on how to acquire a real estate portfolio. At the same time, I even found some of the authors I was reading and participated in their teaching seminars and other events around the country, attending whenever I could.

These groups propelled me and my thinking way beyond what my formal education had given me. At first, I spent a lot of time with the real estate groups. But in my forties, the most significant mentor I found was with our co-author, Dan Kennedy, in private coaching and in his and mastermind group: Titanium.

Working Your Way Up

In the early 2000s, I found Dan through the books he had written. I read everything I could get my hands on. Soon I found out he was part of a group that did a few large events a year. After going to a couple of events, I also discovered Dan had subgroups, which are different levels of mastermind groups we could join, and these met more frequently. Your subgroup level depended on your level of progress in your own company. The highest-level mastermind group is the Titanium Group, consisting of Dan's innermost circle that he leads personally.

In 2008, I was actually at one of those larger events, where I caught Dan Kennedy in the hall during a break. At the time, Dan didn't really know me from anybody else, but I used the moment to make an impression, and he was kind enough to listen to me.

Then, before I stepped away, I said, "You know, I'd love to be in your Titanium group."

Dan was very kind, in reply asking, "Well, who are you working with right now?"

At the time I had another coach who was helping me with public speaking and messaging so I could put together what I was doing with my story and what I do with real estate and business. I shared all this with Dan.

"Good," Dan said. "Stay where you are. Work that with that mentor and that community as deeply as you can. Then, your time will come."

These were the best words I needed to hear. Think about it. Rather than pushing me away, Dan was telling me the truth: get the most out of what you have—then be ready for more at the right time, right place. And you know what? He was absolutely right.

Dan was telling me the truth: get the most out of what you have—then be ready for more at the right time, right place.

Eight years later, in 2016, I applied to Dan's group. I knew I was ready. And Dan accepted me.

When I first started with mastermind groups, I was involved with one at a time, because that's all I could handle. I wasn't ready to take on more.

Over the years, I've appreciated more and more the value of these small groups and the relationships they provide. Today, I do a lot of things on a lot of levels, which means I'm typically a member of multiple groups at a time. Mastermind groups, groups involved in real estate, and others in entrepreneurial businesses—everything from brick and mortar to information marketing. In some groups I'm a veteran; in others, I'm closer to a beginner.

In addition, I usually have one, two, or three personal coaches or mentors who I work with 1:1, every month doing calls where they help me navigate myself, navigate through higher-level thinking, and be more strategic on a bigger level.

Who Should Give You Advice?

Twenty years ago, I was just like many of the entrepreneurs and professionals I speak with: I was making decisions in the dark.

My decision-making was no more sophisticated than consulting with maybe a close family member or a friend or two—that was it. The decisions I considered were based on my experience and on what society generally told me was acceptable or not. That's a very limited way to make a decision.

Most people make decisions in a vacuum like this. If they do ask for advice, it's usually not from peers or people who can give them unbiased advice or the best advice for them.

Perhaps you get advice from a family member or someone in your social circle. Where is their advice coming from? Do they really have the experience to understand you and your decision?

I know many people who, with good intentions, give advice with the goal of helping you achieve more *security*. This is so common. Most people chase security themselves, so don't be

THE POWER OF ASSOCIATION

That's the situation we had in our Freedom Founders mastermind group during March and April 2020, when the pandemic response had shuttered our businesses.

In our regular Zoom calls during that time, many of our members described how at first, they were in a near panic, wondering, "How will our business—and our family—make it through this unprecedented, unplanned-for crisis?"

The collective wisdom and experience of our group provided an incalculable benefit. There was less fear and more proactive leadership. No one felt alone. Everyone was forging a path through uncertain times gaining confidence in sharing the experience and knowledge-sharing in the group. This is why "going solo" is a bad idea. Nothing good happens in a vacuum.

So how to find those peers?

Wisdom Is Everywhere Around You, If You Look for It

Let's start with the obvious: if you're in an industry-specific business, you likely have an industry-specific association. Participate in it.

If you're seeking a strategic association, start with where you are. (Yes, I'm giving you the same advice Dan gave me!) Within any industry association you join, there's always a small subset of people who have already figured out whatever advice you need.

You may be obligated to participate in the industry association for technical training, but, while participating, look for this subset—ideally those who are working toward their freedom. Look for them. They are there.

How do you know? Conversations. You will have to kiss a few frogs. You're looking for those who almost speak a unique language.

It's about attitude – life and business. On the way, you'll meet many complainers. They whine about all of the elements that cause them stress. Those who think differently and operate at a higher level will speak about *opportunities* within the challenges faced. They will express an optimism within the reality of the world as it is, never succumbing to the negativity that pervades so much of the general conversations.

These are the people you should seek. Wisdom takes an investment of time, but it's so well worth it. And as you find this subset tribe, they will lead you to other people and resources that will propel you on a new path. Be prepared to share your own thoughts and experiences. Be willing to be vulnerable. In the right group, with the right people, there will be no judgment – only offers of advice or questions to gain clarity. If you find judgmental or ego-centric individuals, you haven't yet found the quality of community you want. Keep searching.

> ## If you find judgmental or ego-centric individuals, you haven't yet found the quality of community you want. Keep searching.

Don't be afraid to step up and talk to people. Even if you're standing in line, sitting down for a lunch break, or crossing paths in the hall, seek opportunities to intermingle with those who catch your attention.

Have ready a list of questions you want to ask. People like to talk about themselves. Most people also like to help if they have advice to offer.

Look—I'm very much an introvert, so I'm not saying this is easy for me to do. But I forced myself to be a better communicator one-on-one with people, getting to know them a little bit on the surface, then digging in and asking the question on my mind. Questions such as: *What other groups or fields of study do you participate in? Do you have any mentors? What else do you do outside of our specific arena?*

You may have to ask ten people before you find one that says, "Oh, yeah, I'm a part of the EO (Entrepreneur's Organization) group." Or "I'm a part of Freedom Founders."

You've just got to ask. And participate. Do what your peers do and grow outside of your technical specialization.

That's how you start. You've got to start with where you are. Ask, ask, ask. Then, ask some more.

After asking and participating for a few years, learning everything you can from your peers, you may be ready to enter that next-level association we're talking about. For me, it was Dan's Titanium Group. I liked this one because it had a lot of variety: professional practice owners, brick and mortar businesses, coaching and wisdom businesses, writers, marketers, and more.

Once you get to the next level, then it becomes easier to keep going, because you're moving up the ladder, finding more people who are in the same evolutionary process as you.

The peers on your path can help you in good times and bad.

In 2020, when the Covid-19 response hit my groups, our discussion points very quickly focused on how everybody needed to pivot, meaning make some quick alterations to their business model. The dynamics changed overnight, and we all needed to do the same.

It was really great to be in a group where people had those open discussions. Everybody's business is a little bit different, so their strategies may be different. But you really create synergy when you have these discussions and people are competing with their ideas. You'll grab something that's flying through the air and go, "Wow! That just might work—I gotta try it." You likewise get a chance to articulate what you're thinking. You share the seeds of what might be a good idea and then get trusted feedback: "Good idea!" or "Think about adding this to it. Would that work better?"

These discussions give you real-time clarity and the ability to make better, faster, smarter decisions. Decisions you can make with confidence—certainly less risk because you're prevented from making a poor decision when you have the wise counsel of those around you.

That's what I've seen in my groups now, and in my own group, Freedom Founders.

We did what we call a 60-day sprint. We had a town hall virtual meeting every week, Friday at 10:00 AM, for eight consecutive weeks through April and May 2020, during the time when many businesses were in a mandated shut-down by local government.

We used the sprint to strategically optimize our businesses for the shutdown and long-term pandemic response. Figuring out the PPP loans that were being made available by the federal stimulus; considering how to move forward with employees—Layoffs? Furloughs?— and how to virtually lead our staff; learning how to interact and communicate anew with our clients; and more.

There were so many pieces that we needed to discuss. Throughout, there was much thankfulness and gratitude. We realized that nothing is ever as good or bad as we initially might believe. Our tribe got through that time well. And while there was stress in the beginning, the relief was palpable toward the end. Everyone got through it together, and, as a result, took away many great lessons learned.

We survived because of our associations. Our businesses survived. We became better leaders. We learned more about ourselves: about our business efficiencies, our employees, our customers. We created new contingency plans for future disruption.

As I write this a year later, we are all are doing well. Today, with our businesses pretty much running full steam once again, every one of our members is having higher productivity—and, in most cases, with less overhead. At the same time, the level of team culture has improved.

Bottom-line: our associations helped us make the best of a potentially devastating situation.

Your Freedom Mentality

A lot of us feel like if we're not doing something productive – trading time for dollars, getting paid for something – then we're doing nothing. But as you know, trading time for dollars doesn't provide you more freedom. (In fact, high income can be a trap without a transition plan to passive income.) The silver lining is the mandated shutdown gave us two months to focus on strategy, providing a more definitive path to freedom than had we been "productive" or busy during the same time.

From that, our Freedom Founders members discovered our strategic time paid off in dividends, both in the short-term and long-term.

It's the old adage about taking some time to strategically think about your life and your business. It's important *not* to feel like in every moment you've got to be productive, "doing the work" in the business.

That's a mentality that may be new for many of us. We believe that if we are not "working" or "producing" (aka, just "busy"), that we are not productive. There's a guilt attached with taking time off. That's a terrible harness to put on a creative mind.

When it comes to association, there are two types of mentality to be aware of: h*erd mentality* and your *freedom mentality.*

The herd mentality is that most everyone attaches their worth to trading time for dollars. It's what we've been taught by society and our own industries.

The freedom mentality is investing your time—not just trading for dollars—in a strategic way that has an exponentially bigger payoff than what you could earn hour to hour. The payoffs may not always be financial, either, as they can serve your life and lifestyle.

I mention herd mentality because inherent in many livelihoods and associations is a herd mentality. Herd mentality trends toward security, not freedom.

Herd mentality trends toward security, not freedom.

Having a freedom mentality means you're seeking out others who don't always follow the herd. They think bigger about life, living life differently than the herd or the masses. That's what they're about. Having that kind of association emboldens others, if they're not already thinking that way, to think that way—differently than everybody else.

Do you think: *Well, I could never do that. I could never be like that, or have that kind of lifestyle, or have that kind of business.*

Well, why not? Those with a freedom mentality think: *Why not me?*

The mechanics of owning your freedom and benefiting from your associations are important. But so is your mindset, which must be freedom-oriented over herd-oriented.

When your mindset is right, you'd be amazed at the ideation that occurs in these kinds of groups.

Just to give you an example. I was with a group in Nashville in mid-2020. Each member spent thirty minutes in a hot seat. We'd sit in front of the room, share where we were with our business, and ask or answer questions to help get clarity.

Truly, in thirty minutes, I got all the direction that had been eluding me for months prior on a few key challenges. They were challenges in my mind but clearly not in the minds of others who had an outside perspective. I walked in with uncertainty, and I left with a specific set of answers and additional questions that helped me on the path to clarity. Taking the next steps was easy. I had no fear or reticence.

None of the questions or answers were "by the book." There were no "inside the box" moments. For most, it's rare or difficult to find people and ideas that push you toward freedom. But when you find them, you'll achieve the clarity that you would struggle to get otherwise.

Understanding Autonomy: Your Peers on the Path to Freedom

We want to *lean* on one another. We *don't* want to jump on the backs of others and drag everyone down.

To do the former and not the latter, we have to understand autonomy.

When you're with other people who are thinking differently and have already made moves to live differently, you find there's a sense of peace of mind among those peers. The peace comes from their autonomy.

These peers are productive as drivers. They have a mission about them. They want to make an impact. They're not always first and foremost about the money. They already have some profitable enterprise that allows them to keep doing what they're doing.

In general, they have taken a bigger look at life, which gives someone who is new the permission to exit the herd mentality and join their peers on the path to owning freedom.

A big part of our life in society is in seeking permission to be or to do something different. We often have a guilt complex that might be associated with one's parents or perhaps a teacher at school who told you that you're really good at math and you should be an engineer. That influence could've been the key factor in your pursuit of engineering as a profession. But if that's not your thing, then you may be stuck with guilt that's preventing you from switching gears. You'll remain stuck until you get permission to move on.

Your peers (those with a like-minded spirit of freedom) can provide you limitless permission. If it helps you own your freedom, they'll encourage you to pursue it. They'll show you how or why you're stuck. They'll show you what worked well yesterday may not work well today. They'll show you how flexibility and adaptability help you iterate no matter how volatile the economy. And from that permissionand that journeying on a shared path can grow a deep reservoir of confidence.

Confidence is the currency you get from your associations. Confidence without wisdom can be dangerous. Confidence *with* curiosity can work like jet fuel.

> Confidence without wisdom can be dangerous. Confidence *with* curiosity can work like jet fuel.

Curiosity

Lastly, because of my non-traditional career path, many people have asked me what I think makes me unique. What allows me to take a purposeful, active path toward freedom? What allows me to maintain a freedom mindset, to pursue autonomy, to enjoy association?

I reply that the one characteristic or skill I've relied on since the beginning has been my *curiosity*. Especially my curiosity of those who have taken a non-traditional approach to life and business, which compels me to ask them questions.

By asking others questions, I reduce my own blind spots and any prior indoctrination. Conversations, especially those that go beyond the superficial and in which one or both participants are truly curious, can help us do this.

That's why I like interviews. Whether I'm interviewing our Freedom Founders members during our meetings or on our podcasts, "The Dentist Freedom Blueprint" and "Own Your Freedom", the back and forth of an interview helps me see something that previously I didn't know I was missing.

If I could leave you one action item from this chapter, it's this: Just be inquisitive. This works the same whether you're talking to a Fortune 500 CEO or the couple next door who has a garden you admire.

Don't be hesitant to step up and get to know someone on a deeper level. Be curious. By the time you learn to do it the right way, with the right people, you will be well on your way to owning your freedom.

To tune in to our podcasts visit
www.DentistFreedomBlueprint.com or
www.OwnYourFreedomPodcast.com

CHAPTER 5

THE CRITICALITY OF INDEPENDENT THINKING

BY DAN S. KENNEDY

Nothing more precedes financial losses and goal failures than **Loss of Mind**. Not loss of mind to dementia or similar incapacity, but to Group-Think. Partly thanks to social media – both its exerted control over what is and isn't *allowable* information and opinion, and by its facilitation of peer pressure – we live immersed in more Group-Think than at any time in recent history, perhaps requiring reaching back to the times of the Reformation or into totalitarian regimes for precedents.

All sorts of critical, analytical, and skeptical thinking now get quickly shouted down with simplistic intimidatory labels. In October

2020, Michelle Obama said, "**The *discussion of* crime waves in urban cities is <u>racist</u>**." This *should* have triggered consensus outrage from *all* in the free media, political leaders of both parties, academia, and every citizen. It's *not* just an obvious block to solving a problem; if you can't talk about it "legally," you can't work on fixing it. It is more. <u>It is a **totalitarian** premise</u>. (Look up "totalitarian" in the dictionary, *please*.) It is an Elite *dictating* what is *acceptable ("legal") thought;* discussion; reporting… to the media, to us. That she thinks that what is discussed should be controlled, dictated, governed with prohibitions is bad enough. That she said so out loud, in public, is *terrifying*. This is *exactly* how China and Russia operate.

Intimidation – overt and subtle – against dissent from acceptable, commonly accepted Group-Think is no longer incidental. I can find you new examples occurring daily. It is an epidemic.

GROUP-THINK ABOUT MONEY CAN BE HARMFUL TO YOUR WEALTH

One of the areas of life and information flow most controlled by Group-Think is "money" – finance, investing, wealth. This may not be the area where it is most dangerous to the entire society, but it is very dangerous to you, as you go about putting your financial "castle" in order, as you want it to be. The suppression of your independent critical thinking by near-unanimously promoted, promulgated, and insisted upon Group-Think puts you at *financial risk by omission*. The more limited and "boxed in" you are about the options, opportunities, tools, and methods you might use for your personal, individual purposes related to finances, the more at risk you are to harm by omitting, possibly not even understanding or considering best alternatives for your financial goals. With that in mind, here is a piece I wrote for an issue of my Wealth Report, exclusively distributed to Members of Dr. Phelps's Freedom Founders:

LED BY THE NOSE

"Led by the nose" refers to the way "difficult" bulls and horses are led: a pole with a loop of chain is used, the chain wrapped around the soft portion of the lip and/or nose, so the critter is distracted by it, and follows along without resisting.

A simple, visible "secret" was recently, succinctly suggested to me by my partner in multi-unit, residential real estate properties. He said that in a week of watching Fox Business, CNBC, and Bloomberg, he noticed that *they are all "trying to get you to do **one** thing; the same thing."* This IS an interesting observation, given that every majority is almost always wrong, especially about money. Despite a lot of their advertisers promoting gold bullion, gold and silver bulk coins and numismatic coins, they almost never interview experts or "believers" in this category of assets. Despite some of their advertisers promoting real estate investing, directly or via REITs, they almost never interview experts in this category. When they do talk about real estate, it is usually broadly, in home construction or sales statistics, then relate it to The One Thing & The Same Thing they promote: the stock market. Next, consider "financial professionals": CFPs, financial advisors, money-under-management folk. Ninety percent steer to The One Thing & The Same Thing, too. Many also steer to insurance and annuity products, index funds, ETF's, virtually all linked to The One Thing & The Same Thing, too. There is logic to this, of course. "The Market" is the most familiar, most reported on, most promoted by media. To attract viewers, listeners, or readers or to sell "investing," it is convenient to hitch your wagon to the biggest star easily seen in the sky. And, to be fair about it, direct investing in stocks and "packaged" stock market investments have legitimate purposes. However, the relentless, myopic, blatantly promotional focus on The One Thing & The Same Thing is also a danger to your financial independence and security.

Planned, methodical, dogged implementation of a personal, customized strategy properly incurring no more risk than is necessary to achieve your goals, and focused on establishing replacement income more so than "fancy" short-term big gains can be *oh-so BORING*. But "SEX" SELLS. They can make their One Thing exciting, minute by minute, day by day. A "new" or "next" big, bright shiny thing you don't want to miss out on, do you? It has "action," like gambling in the casino. Every "golfing buddy" brags about his wins and keeps his losses to himself. Every stock market investing shill has *three* such stories. All this is seductive. Alluring. "*Mind Sex.*"

One of the most interesting lessons I've learned about growing sustainable businesses is that **the overwhelming majority of success comes from the disciplined implementation of BORING strategies and methods, to their maximum effectiveness.** Consistently successful entrepreneurs, CEO's, marketers, ad copywriters, etc., have **"formulas" they stick with, with boring consistency.** Yes, the Great Innovator or Inventor occasionally wins big. Somewhat like the singer/recording artist who is a "one hit wonder." But if you play the odds, you'll play by formula, and you'll be more committed to boring implementation than to invention. Investing has never seemed much different to me.

This is why "association" is so very, very important.

Truth is, no one can completely escape the gravitational pull of Group-Think, so *carefully picking* the groups you associate with, directly, or indirectly via the media you most consistently consume is vital.

We are hard-wired to be social and tribal creatures, which produces *instinctual* behavior that is extremely difficult to switch off. It was wired in for our protection, because once upon a time there were very big predators roaming around, so hunting, fetching water, even living in a cave alone was too dangerous; tribes and communities formed. Self-preservation and desire for safety are super-powerful instincts. This <u>makes us</u> seek the acceptance and approval of the tribe(s), community(ies), and peer group(s) we enter and become "members" of – and *that* motivates Group-Think. *That* makes opposition to Group-Think unnatural and difficult.

If, as a kid, your family moves from Houston, Texas to Boston, Massachusetts, it won't take very many days at your new school before you are begging and demanding that your parents replace your cowboy boots with *acceptable* shoes. If an older kid raised in a conservative, traditional-values family goes to an extremely "Left" – liberal, west or east coast university, when he or she comes home for Thanksgiving, the parents paying the tab may be shocked at the ideas they hear coming out of their son's or daughter's mouth. Naturally, the college student will have "moved" to *acceptable* Group-Think dominant with the new group they've joined. You do <u>not</u> need to be young to be so affected; it is an ever-present danger (or opportunity) at any and every age.

I say OPPORTUNITY because, if you understand the power of the gravitational pull of the Group-Think of different groups and tribes, you can seek out and select ones to become part of, with Group-Think in sync with your values, ideals, interests, and ambitions. You can make the gravitational pull your ally instead of your opponent!

You can also pick tribes where a lot of independent thought and varied thought within a large frame is encouraged – not squashed. Where questions are welcome. Where a narrow, tight dogma isn't threatened by questions or differences. There ARE such tribes – you have to look for them. And please get this: it is okay to know what environment and kind of association opportunities you are looking for, and to accept nothing less.

A long-ago friend and mentor told me his story of growing up in rural Alabama, dreaming of going to the University of Alabama because he idolized Coach "Bear" Bryant. But he also was firmly fixated on becoming a millionaire. When he reached the right age, he traveled to the University for a campus visit, and asked his counselor/guide "What classes do you have to teach me how to become a millionaire?" When the academic laughed out loud at the idea and said, "Son, we don't have classes about *that*," my friend left immediately.

We aren't living in prehistoric times at constant risk of being dinner for dinosaurs 'n dragons; you do NOT need to join the first tribe you bumble into, that will have you!

What CONTROLS What We BECOME?

The great successful philosopher Earl Nightingale said "We *become* what we think about most." A good joke about that, said by many guys, was "well if that's the case, I'd be a girl." Or: "I'd be a cheeseburger." But gags aside, Earl was definitely onto something. **_Inevitably_, "association + interests" LEAD you toward certain achieved realities (good or bad) <u>and</u> they magnetically ATTRACT what is**

needed to achieve those realities. Since "association + interests" control what you think about most – bingo!

To be specific about this for a moment, consider the matter of FREEDOM, supported by financial freedom. You are most likely to achieve it by prizing it and thinking about it *a lot*; by having interests and associations that facilitate such thoughts. FREE individuals achieve freedom as their reality and become free by thinking about it; what it means (to them); how to achieve it – *a lot*. This is, of course, NOT the dominant interest and chief "work" of most tribes and peer groups you might find yourself in. You have to acknowledge that and *move*. You are *not* a tree rooted into a spot in the ground.

CHAPTER 6

PRINCIPLE №3:

WEALTH IS WHAT YOU OWN, NOT WHAT YOU DO

BY DR. DAVID PHELPS

"There is only one success: to be able
to live your life in your own way."

Christopher Morley

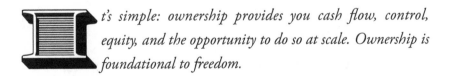 t's simple: ownership provides you cash flow, control, equity, and the opportunity to do so at scale. Ownership is foundational to freedom.

FREEDOM QUESTIONS:

....

What do you *own* that's generating you wealth?

Wealth is created by what you own, not what you do. That's a fact—one that reminds me of a story I've heard Dan tell.

When Dan was a young adult, he was curious about the wealthy, asking anybody he encountered who he thought was rich how they got that way. For his first and only "real" job where he was employed by someone else, Dan was a territory sales rep for a Los Angeles-based book publishing company.

In a meeting at one of the principal's Malibu beach house, Dan's curiosity surfaced again. "How'd you get so rich?" Dan asked. "And how do I?"

"Well," the principal replied, "We own this circus. Ownership is the key to wealth."

"And how do I get rich?"

The principal put it bluntly: "You *won't* get rich. We won't let you. We owners will never let any of you circus monkeys make anywhere near our income, let alone have any equity. Ultimately, we'll sell this company for a boatload of money, a big multiple of its income."

Dan persisted, "But how do I get rich, too?"

The principal considered Dan for a moment, before telling him a truth that's stuck with Dan ever since.

"You can't sell a job for a multiple of your income," the principal said. "Think about that. No job can give you a multiple of your income for the job. You're trading time for dollars, and nothing more. The work you do is not leverageable or scalable, so you need to learn how assets work—about the assembly of assets worth more together than apart. Then leverage rather than work. That's wealth—which is never *just* income."

The assembly of assets worth more together than apart.

In that moment there at the Malibu beach house, Dan didn't understand everything the principal had said. That would take a few more years of learning and experience. But Dan walked away with a profound lesson, which he's found to be true ever since: wealth is ownership.

Wealth is What You Own

This chapter is the book's centerpiece. Here we make the case for ownership: what it is, why it's so central to your freedom, why it's so important to everyone I know and work with, and how my understanding of it has evolved over the years.

Few of us ever learn "wealth is what you own, *not* what you do" in school. Whether in high school, college, or a professional school, the teachers teach us about *doing*. At every level of our education system, the focus is on what you're going to *do* when you graduate. Learn to do something well so that you can make money doing it. Earn a living, create security—that's the outcome of education in a nutshell.

Even if you earn $1,000 an hour as a high-priced litigation attorney in New York City, or as a cardiac surgeon in LA, you're still limited by your labor. While you make a lot of dollars per hour, you're still merely trading your time for dollars.

Trading time for dollars is something we all must do for some portion of our working life (unless you're the beneficiary of a trust fund at an early age). There is always a *sacrifice period* we must go through because we don't just come out of the gate owning assets or having a high income.

In working with a couple on their blueprint day, we'll use a tool I call the "Freedom Curve," which plots their freedom over the course of their career. My premise is that in the *sacrifice period* at the bottom end of the curve, we're not just trading time for dollars, we're also building momentum in a *career that leads to ownership*. (The goal? The "freedom point," where you finally transition to owning your freedom.)

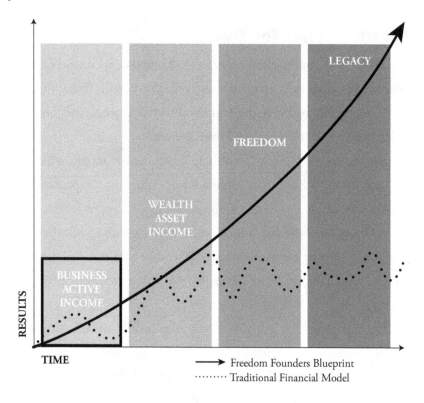

If you are a business owner or professional practice owner, you may feel stuck at the bottom of the curve. Stuck trading time for dollars, but looking for a way to earn more. You might think, "OK, if I want to increase my income, increase my security, and increase my wealth, then I just need to work harder and faster and enhance my skill set." That means if you're a surgeon, a dentist, an architect, a lawyer, a consultant, or a professional business owner of some kind, you're going to continue your specialized education. Learn something new to sell something new. This is a good move. But the improvement on the Freedom Curve is only linear if we stop there.

Continuing education in your profession, even if it provides new income opportunities, is still a linear improvement—for two reasons.

First, there are only so many hours in a week. Even if you're making a thousand dollars an hour, as we said, you're still limited. You can't bend the Freedom Curve a whole lot more once you've maxed out your dollars per hour.

Second, if something happens to you, you're out of luck! That's part of the thinking behind our *Principle #5: Invest in Your Transferable Skill Sets*. No business—or anything in life—can survive as just one of one. Being the sole producer, trading your hours for dollars, means you become very dependent on your ability to continue to produce. When something happens to you, your industry, or the marketplace— such as a black swan event like the Covid-19 pandemic—your income could shrink from a thousand dollars an hour to zero dollars. You don't have control over these circumstances. But you do have control over the duration of your sacrifice period.

Linear improvement is where we as a society focus. Few of us learn to explore what it means to own other assets that produce income; to create or build wealth without us having to be involved in that asset on a daily basis; to not have to show up for an eight-hour workday.

Exponential improvement requires ownership or control of tangible assets (business, real estate, or equipment that you might lease to others to use). You're no longer just trading time for dollars but rather creating wealth exponentially for your time invested. You are transitioning from active labor-produced income to asset-produced income. The former is entirely dependent on your exchange of your time for money. The latter is sustainable annuity income from an acquired or created tangible asset.

After decades of working with mentors and mastermind groups, reading every book I could get my hands on, accumulating experience with a lot of trial and error, and passing on my knowledge to a new generation of owners pursuing freedom, I've found a few concepts are helpful in understanding the principle of ownership.

If you want your ownership to make your wealth exponential, it helps to understand:

* Leverage
* Participations
* Good debt
* Debt snowballing
* Equity geometry
* Geographic arbitrage
* Cash flow on demand

More on these concepts ahead. And visit
www.OwnYourFreedomBook.com/Resources to
learn more details on these topics. It's free of charge
and my gift to you for investing in yourself!

My First Asset

First, I should give you a story of my own—how I first realized ownership can make wealth *exponential*, a phenomenon I experienced while in college and dental school.

You see, in college, I waited tables. Nights and weekends. That's how I made the money to help pay my way through school and afford tuition, books, room, board, and what little else I might want on the outside. Whatever I needed or wanted, I had to earn. Waiting tables was a good way to earn because I could make pretty decent money and I had flexible hours for classes.

In my free time, I read books on the stock market, real estate, and how to be a good steward of your assets—not that I had any, but I was curious. Of everything I read, real estate made the most sense. It was something I could do myself, without the buffer of a Wall Street rep; historically, it had less volatility than the stock market; it was tangible, not something that could disappear forever overnight; and it was something that I felt I could control.

In 1980, during my first year of dental school, I convinced my dad to be my financier, my private capital investor, if you will, and brought him to Dallas, where I was going to school at the Baylor College of Dentistry (as it was known at the time).

My pitch to my dad was simple: "I'm going to be here in Dallas for at least four years of dental school before I graduate. So I can do one of two things: I can pay rent for four years and come away with nothing more than just having had a place to live. Or we—*we* being the key word here—could invest in a property, which I will also gladly manage. And if you could just put up the down payment and your credit (because I had neither), then together we may control an asset that produces cash flow and builds equity during those four years."

My dad was willing, but he wasn't going to blindly hand over credit and money to do it. In it together as business partners, we looked at properties together. We then shared ownership, and I was the manager. After paying all expenses and the mortgage with rent paid by the co-tenants, we split any profit fifty-fifty.

But here's the key. In owning that property for about three and a half years, when I graduated from dental school because I was going to move on, I saw the need to sell the property because I could no longer be there to manage it. We put it on the market and we split about fifty thousand dollars in capital gain net profit. For me, that's twenty-five thousand in 1983. That was a heck of a lot of money for a kid coming out of school who didn't have any money.

Then, as I looked closer at what happened, I realized my tip money—when I added up the number of hours that I worked waiting tables—probably averaged fifteen dollars an hour.

Looking at the hours I put in to find, acquire, and manage the property, there was a 10X ratio for my time. In other words, I made 10 times more per hour by owning that asset than compared to my hourly work waiting tables. That fact got my absolute attention.

I made 10 times more per hour by owning that asset.

My first taste of exponential wealth lingered with me. Like my newly graduated peers, I had the thought, "I'm going to be a dentist! So I'll make more money as a dentist than I would doing anything else." Still, there was something about owning this property that had proved to me that owning assets could be a bigger wealth builder than hourly work.

At the time, I didn't know that down the road, I would leave the practice because of my daughter's health situation—that actually this ownership of assets would provide me my "Plan B," a way to segue from my hourly work at a time when I needed to the most. And that without ownership of outside-the-practice investment assets, I would've been stuck without any good options. These moments came later.

So what did I do with the $25,000? I leveraged it.

Leverage

We must understand the proper and wise use of leverage, as it's the surest method I've found to generate exponential wealth. But leverage inherently comes with some risk, so understanding how to evaluate that risk is essential.

I could have taken $25,000 and tried to buy a property at that time in all cash, just applying the 25k lump to one property. Then, sure, I'd have no debt. But even back in 1983, $25,000 was not going to buy a very good property. It would have bought a lower economic area property, which would have had issues, and would have attracted an inconsistent tenant base. In short, a poor investment candidate.

My dad and I had used leverage to buy our first property. We had used my dad's credit, leveraging a 20 percent down payment to finance 80 percent of the property's purchase price. The second time around, I wanted to do the same thing, using the 25k as leverage to purchase other properties.

The traditional way to finance a home is with a mortgage lender. For me, coming out of dental school, I was not creditworthy enough to go to the bank. I didn't have enough vested time in my new career as a dentist for a lender to finance me.

Financing with Good Credit

For those who have good credit, businesses with years in the marketplace, and a track record of income, lenders are willing to help you finance. Even in 2020, in the midst of the volatile Covid-19 pandemic, lenders' doors were open. A lawyer, for example, would have no trouble buying five $100,000 homes with bank loans. The bank would even package them up into a bundle.

One of our Freedom Founders members did just that. He bought fifteen properties at once. Sure, he's been in business for a decade-plus, he's in his mid-to-late 40s, with a relatively decent net worth from two businesses. So he's leveraging with a lender because he wants to build more growth. Fifteen in one shot. That's doable if you have the credit, collateral, and track record—it's a sure way to achieve exponential wealth.

Instead of financing with a mortgage lender, I had to use leverage in two other ways: find a seller who could be the bank for me, or take over payments on the existing loan.

In the former, I found sellers who had equity in their property, who were close to free and clear, and who would actually agree to *be the bank* for me. I signed a note and mortgage in favor of the seller, which obligated me to make the monthly payment to them in order to own the rental asset.

These sellers were willing to finance me because I showed up in person, shared about my stable career as a dentist, and gained their confidence. I had to earn a high degree of trust, especially because in this case they're actually transferring the title to me.

The other way I leveraged was I took over payments on the existing loan. I took title to these properties and agreed to pay the existing bank loan that the prior owner had.

Again, this leverage is a little bit risky for the seller because they'd like to leave their house with no liability attached—because, obviously, if I quit paying, then they're still on the hook. But that's what I had to do. I learned to be creative and resourceful.

Not every seller was motivated enough to be interested. But some were. I might make 10 or 12 offers before I'd get one seller to agree.

Over the next fifteen years, I steadily acquired a portfolio of over thirty-five properties, with an average price point of sixty-five thousand dollars.

Over the next fifteen years, I acquired a portfolio of over thirty-five properties.

Multiply 35 x $65,000, and I controlled $2,275,000 of total property value. I had the benefit of tax depreciation offsets against the positive rental cash flow (not much at first) and the inflation hedge. In addition, I used the tenant's rental payments with some of my discretionary active income to "snowball" down the debt on this portfolio, getting most of the $2-plus million portfolio free of debt in fifteen years (more on that ahead). Two million and change is a heckuva lot of equity—much more than I could comfortably save in fifteen years as a dentist.

Leverage allowed me to buy thirty-five properties in fifteen years. More importantly, I was acquiring strong assets that, once paid off of debt, would provide strong cash flow. Without leverage, I probably would have bought just three, maybe four at most.

So the ability to leverage and acquire more of these assets—purchased correctly, acquired correctly with the right metrics, and managed properly—allowed me to grow my wealth exponentially. At the point that I sold my practice in 2005, my net worth was 5X the equity from my practice sale, all from the real estate acquisition and leverage over those twenty years. Real estate (and the cash flow) set me free.

Participations

A multiplier that I did not recognize or embrace until later in life is the use of participations—combining forces with other investors to create synergy in an investment deal or opportunity.

What we are taught in school is that "if it is to be, it has to be me." In other words, whatever our goal, we had to be in control. We designed it, we built out the plan, and we carried it out. This is what I call the "John Wayne rugged individualist."

But in life, in the real world of business, collaboration with others (See: Principle #2: The Power of Association) is the fast track to collapse time and build net worth.

A framework that I teach to my Freedom Founders members is the *Anatomy of a Deal.*

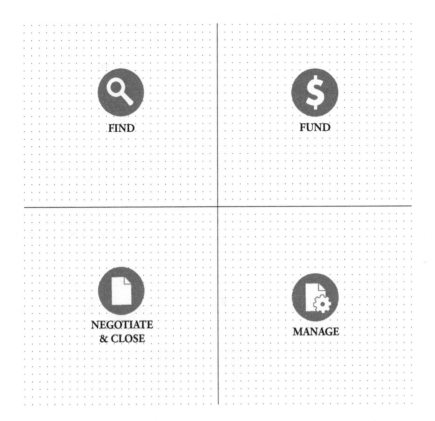

First, someone has to find or identify a potential investment opportunity. This can be someone who markets for specific types of investments as a business or is connected to a database, such as the multiple listing service for real estate (MLS) or other exchange platforms.

Secondly, someone must have the experience to negotiate and close the transaction with the seller. This is a higher level of expertise than finding a possible opportunity.

Third, financing and capital must be arranged to close on the sale transaction.

Finally, and often the most neglected part of a deal structure, is the management. The person who has the capability of managing the asset for profit or cash flow is a very important aspect of the success of the deal.

The takeaway is this: you can control all four components of a deal, investment, or opportunity, OR you can bring to the table that which is the best trade for you, assuming you complement the assets and/or the expertise of the other player(s).

For example, as I started out in my investing career, I controlled all four aspects. I learned how to find, negotiate, and close the opportunity. I had to construct the financing, often by taking over existing financing of the seller and/or getting the seller to finance the greater amount of their remaining equity. And, yes, I also managed the property. I didn't know any other way.

Fast forward a decade. Through my network associations that grew year by year, I had others bring me investment opportunities (quadrant 1, "find" the deal). I was good at negotiating the terms of sale and taking the deal to closing (quadrant 2, "negotiate and close"). At that point, I was often able to contribute funds necessary to close—becoming a more passive investor (quadrant 3, "fund" the deal). How about quadrant 4 ("manage the deal")? Because I wanted to be passive at this stage in my life, I found another party who I would joint venture the management with and provide a backend equity stake in the deal.

As a result of participations, I have been able to be involved in many more investments than if I had controlled all four quadrants. I used what I could bring to any particular deal and collaborated with one or two others which allowed me to scale my investments and leverage what I could do best. Most importantly, I used my time and experience where it mattered most.

Good Debt

Regarding financial leverage, we have to shout out to Dave Ramsey, who obviously has a big platform. Dave's a great leader and voice out there against what I call bad debt, consumer debt. He's so anti-debt because many have gotten into too much lifestyle consumption debt, which can be a terrible drag on their future.

What I'm talking about with leverage is good debt.

For most of us, debt (school loans) was the only way to achieve our educational goals. With real estate and business, debt is the way you get into that business or acquire that asset. If you use that debt wisely, then you can control up to five times more than you could without leverage. You can expand a business or a real estate portfolio, as I did, much faster because of the leverage. That was very useful debt for me. It can't be variable rate or short term. You don't buy long-term assets with short-term debt. It's got to be long-term, fixed-rate debt.

For example: when the credit markets constrict during a recession, you don't want to have the bank call your lines of credit. Often during credit recessions, short-term lines of credit are called by the lender, which puts the borrower into a predicament that many times cannot be overcome.

Good debt works because I own a relatively small percent of the equity in a property, but I control 100 percent of the property. At the same time, tenant payments are building equity by paying down the loan mortgage (amortization of debt) plus any market appreciation. I get 100 percent of the benefits of ownership with only a small portion of my own money involved—this is the advantage of good debt.

Once you have acquired a nice portfolio of leveraged properties with solid cash flow beyond the property expenses and debt payments, a technique called debt snowballing can be used to build more equity and systematically begin paying off the good debt. This is but one strategy that can be used. It made sense for me, but other strategies that I know can obtain the same objective of freedom depending on the particular circumstances and time goals of any one person or couple.

> I get 100 percent of the benefits of ownership with only a small portion of my own money involved – this is the advantage of good debt.

Debt Snowballing to Pay off My Next 35 Properties

As I steadily acquired the thirty-five properties, I was getting cash flow from two places: my dental practice work and payments from my tenants.

I used my tenant payments to pay the debt. But I also used income from my job, taking what discretionary money I did have out of the dental practice to make additional payments against the principal balance on the loan.

I started what we now call debt snowballing, meaning paying down the mortgage balance faster than the actual scheduled payment term. This would allow me to pay off the debt of one property much faster and then use the additional cash flow from that property to pay down the next one even faster, thus creating the snowball effect to pay down the next properties even faster.

For example: let's say you bought a house with a mortgage minimum monthly payment of $600 a month. If you add another

$250 to your monthly payment and put it toward the principle, you're paying extra money against the mortgage. Doing so will pay off a thirty-year mortgage in fifteen years, or half the time.

With the thirty-five properties, I added a couple thousand dollars to the paydown each month until I completely freed up one property, then I would go on to the next. With the first property free and clear, with no debt, the net cash flow from it would increase substantially, which I'd then put toward paying off the next property.

Suddenly the first property is a multiplier. It allows me to pay off the second property even faster. As soon as the second is paid off, it likewise becomes a multiplier, quickly paying off the third, then the fourth, and so on.

That's debt snowballing. The more debt you pay off, the more the properties become multipliers. The more multipliers, the more ownership and the more equity (net worth). Doing this allowed me to pay off the vast majority of my thirty-five properties in only fifteen years.

The kicker? As with my first asset (the rental with my father), I spent less than a tenth of time than I spent trading time for dollars as a dentist. Even though my business became more and more successful producing transactional income, the net worth or wealth increase of the practice only grew to about 20 percent of what the real estate net worth became. I leveraged what I learned from that first rental property and, as a result, increased my net worth and passive income by 5X.

Equity Geometry: Growing It in Four Ways

A good rental property today in the right market may average in acquisition costs about $100,000 - $165,000, depending on the market. If I had the money, I could pay the hundred grand and own it free and clear. Or I could take that same hundred thousand dollars and divide it $20,000 apiece over five properties that are also worth a hundred thousand dollars, financing the remaining 80 percent. Doing so, I'd own five properties with essentially the same amount of equity, that 20 percent at the top.

The benefit of equity (net worth) is that you can grow it over time. You don't have to buy it outright. We thus build wealth in equity positions in four ways.

First is acquiring an asset or property that's undervalued at a discount to the market. Why was it undervalued? Maybe it hadn't been taken care of. Maybe the seller had financial issues or family or job issues—whatever the reason, there's motivation for them to sell a property at some discount to the market. Even a 10 or 15 percent markdown is a discount on the market. That's one way to acquire what we call immediate or instant equity.

Second, equity could come from actually adding some value to a property. You could be a better manager, optimizing the income from the rental property. Or you might do some cosmetic fixup to make it look better and attract a higher quality tenant who would pay a little bit more in rent. That's going to add value to it, which increases your equity position.

Third, there are natural appreciation or inflation factors, which will add to the property value. That's the inflation hedge of tangible assets, which I believe will be a major factor in the remainder of this decade and longer.

Fourth, there's the amortization of paying down the debt, which the tenant is doing by paying it down through their rent.

The growth of equity comes from:

1. Buying at a discount
2. Adding value
3. Inflation and market appreciation
4. Amortization of debt

Knowing these four ways to build equity, here's a question: would you rather be doing this for one property or five at the same time?

What made my portfolio successful at a relatively young age is that I was growing equity in these four ways in at least five properties at the same time—plus the fact that I was debt snowballing, then reinvesting in another five properties, then another five, and so on.

The opportunity you have now is to start building equity as early as possible, in as many ways as possible, in as many properties as possible.

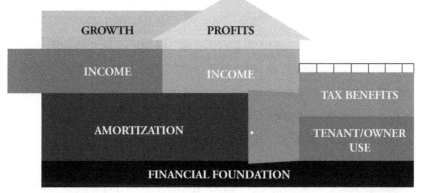

Diagram courtesy of Pete Fortunato

The benefits of real estate.

Geographic Arbitrage

In speaking to entrepreneurs all around the country, many ask, *How is location a factor in where we purchase real estate?*

Location is very important because it's one of the key metrics we use to evaluate whether an asset is the right acquisition or not.

There are certainly areas of the country where our leverage model would not work. For example, volatile and expensive areas like California or Arizona, some parts of Florida, the East Coast, and New York City—wherever the prices skyrocket when times are good but dramatically drop when there's a reset in the marketplace. Such volatility in real estate doesn't make for a good asset, so we avoid those markets.

Typically, we talk about the Midwest, the Rust Belt, and the southeast areas of the country, where the market value of the kind of assets we invest in are still very modest and inherently have less volatility. These properties are most conducive to this model.

We're not talking about multimillion-dollar properties. For single-family homes, we're talking about properties typically in a range today of $80,000-$160,000.

Location is one of several metrics that become more and more important the higher up you go in asset classes. Single-family homes are the simplest place to start acquiring properties. But if you gain momentum, it's not unusual for people to invest money in additional real estate asset classes. The higher up you go in the asset classes (commercial), the more complexity you encounter.

For example, demographic area is even more important in syndications, where you've got a deal sponsor manager who is investing your money with other people's money into a single larger facility like a self-storage, a multifamily apartment, or other commercial buildings.

Commercial real estate assets require a much higher-level approach, complexity of due diligence, and economic underwriting than single-family assets. A novice investor should never attempt to undertake such vetting on his or her own.

A few other metrics to consider:

* Market saturation or demand for that asset class
* Track record of the deal sponsor
* The "essential nature" of the asset

Market saturation or demand for that asset class

For commercial properties, one must determine, through demographic studies and analysis, how much current demand for the use (rental) of the asset exists and what are future estimated projections for use. For example, the multi-family apartment market was red hot for a number of years post-2008 recession. At some point (and in many markets at the time this book was published in 2021), demand for multi-family reached saturation. Yet with "hot money" (Federal Reserve and U.S. Treasury debt stimulation), chasing yield (higher returns than conventional bonds, CDs, or T-Bills) there appears to be no end in sight for more development and rising prices of current assets. Investor beware!

Knowing when and how to "move" one's money from one asset class to another, from equities (ownership) to debt (being the bank as a lender) and when to go to cash are the skillsets that a financial advocate needs to understand. This knowledge and experience can be accessed quickly through high-caliber, high net worth groups, such as Freedom Founders, where one can rely on the experience and access of others instead of trying to re-invent the wheel on their own. "Going solo" will require a great deal of time, lost opportunity costs, and actual monetary losses by getting involved in the wrong investment at the wrong time. Sometimes it simply pays to invest in yourself and your own future instead of trying to do it all yourself. Another lesson to "take to the bank."

Track record of the deal sponsor

If the goal is truly "passive" annuity (sustainable) asset-based cash flow, then the investor is going to have to rely on someone else to manage the asset. That's the whole point of recurring revenue not based on the activity of the beneficiary of that income. This is in contrast to what most of us learned growing up. We were taught that "if it was to be, it had to be me." That's great when we want to be involved and active, such as in a business or professional practice. But at some point, if we want to orchestrate our financial future and base that future on capital assets (Main Street vs. Wall Street), then the "who" is just as important as the "what."

Most novice investors who I meet don't understand the importance of vetting the deal sponsor. Most novice investors are far too trusting and wouldn't know how to vet or what questions should be asked. The novice investor believes it would be an affront or disrespectful to ask the "hard questions" that absolutely should be asked before turning one's hard-earned money over to someone else to manage. And that is precisely why we read time and time again about a manager or promoter who took a lot of investor money and went belly up or outright defrauded the investors (ever heard of Bernie Madoff? He took the money from many celebrities who you would think would know better. It happens to the best—but that's not an excuse for you!).

Over the years, simply by being involved in multiple real estate, business, and investor mastermind groups, I have curated a vast network of potential investment opportunities. The keyword is "potential." Before I jump in with anyone, I have my securities attorney (the same one who vets all of the investment deal flow for Freedom Founders), run full background checks on the principals in the business. Do you do that? My guess is no.

Is that it? Not at all. If the background check is clear (and, trust me, that often turns up details that you would absolutely want to know about someone's history), the next step is to evaluate the track record or performance of the principal (deal sponsor) in the specific asset class that he or she promotes. The due diligence checklist that we use in Freedom Founders is four pages long! Yes! It is THAT important!

Here's where the rubber meets the road. There's a saying that "Everyone is a genius in a bull market," meaning, it's hard not to be successful to some degree in a market where everything is going up including the economy, low unemployment, and more. That's the market we enjoyed from roughly 2012 to early 2020, when the Covid-19 pandemic began. But even post-pandemic, the market has picked back up in many ways due to the massive government debt-stimulus bailouts. Is this real? I think not. Warren Buffett says it best: "It's only when the tide goes out that you know who's been swimming naked."

I just don't really want to be in the same water with those people—do you?

The essential nature of the asset

The coronavirus pandemic elicited new meaning to the word "essential." If the government deemed your business services or products as "essential" during the pandemic, you and your business were allowed to remain open while the rest (the majority) were told, "you must close." I won't get into the politics of this decision by politicians who often didn't follow their own mandated regulations ("rules for me and rules for thee" – you can probably guess where I stand). The point is, how "essential" is your business and how "essential" are your investment assets?

Here are a few examples: Grocery stores remained open, at least the large chains. Airlines were allowed to continue to operate, violating the 6-foot social distance science. But if you were the owner of a hair salon, restaurant, bar, gym, dental practice, or a whole host of other small businesses, you were told, "you must close."

The pandemic was actually a very good test case for the resiliency of our capital investments (real estate). Hotels, hospitality, and tourism – deemed non-essential – are still having great difficulty today, well over a year after the pandemic began and even with mask and business closure mandates lifted. Meanwhile, some retail commercial properties took a short-term hit, when small business retail tenants were hurting. Some of these retail centers have come back and are on track—others, depending on the geography, debt structure and market-savvy of the deal sponsor, may not be doing so well. Senior assisted living facilities, due to the nature of their clients (age and susceptibility to the virus), experienced some significant reductions in cash flows. However, once again, the geographic and deal sponsor strength have brought the best of these facilities through the pandemic, and many are, once again, producing solid returns.

Single-family residential in the right geographic and demographic regions with the right manager left only a slight (2-3 percent) reduction in cash flow, mostly only during the early months of the pandemic. Multi-family, self-storage, and mobile home park communities, again, in the right geographic and demographic regions with the right deal sponsor, had very little in temporary interruption of cash flows.

My question to you is, "How well do your financial investment assets (Wall Street) perform during an economic downturn?" One will experience not only a diminution of dividend payments but also a loss of principal investment from a downturn in stocks, bonds, and annuities.

Cash Flow on Demand

So *why must we own*? Why are the methods of leverage, debt snowballing, and more so essential in achieving ownership? It's simple: ownership provides you cash flow, equity, and the opportunity to do so at scale. It is not dependent on our time—if we do this with a blueprint plan.

Cash flow is the desired outcome. It's why we take the time to purchase an asset that meets our metrics, to build equity, and to repeat that enough times until our assets provide cash flow that meets our freedom point on the Freedom Curve. Because enough cash flow means you're free: free to do what you want, when you want, and to not have to worry about clocking in at the office to pay your bills.

Every member who starts with Freedom Founders needs, at some level, to invest further in capital assets. Owning and optimizing assets helps move a member to their freedom point faster than the course they'd been on.

Once you hit your freedom point, these assets provide sustainability, despite major volatility like the Covid-19 pandemic.

Once you hit your freedom point, these assets provide sustainability, despite major volatility like the Covid-19 pandemic. Here are two reasons why:

First, the asset you own should produce a regular sustainable income *without you*, the owner of the asset, actually having to do a lot of work like you would in a regular job.

Second, by owning assets, the equity portion of the assets should keep pace with inflation. If you're afraid of the cost of living in your future, with expenses like healthcare or taxes going up, know that these assets will typically rise in value and cash flow along with the rate of inflation. The rise protects the asset's earning power.

The results of hitting one's freedom point are always life-changing.

For the business owners I work with, as soon as they see how they can achieve freedom much faster than expected, they're relieved. It's palpable. The epiphany removes stress and produces more certainty for the future. The relief and certainty make them different people because they're not stuck wondering, "Do I have to keep working like this forever?"

A big part of the certainty comes from us showing our members how they are progressing so that, when they hit their numbers, they can be confident in making the call to step away. They see the big picture, how it fits with the numbers, and gain the certainty that they have enough with the assets they have invested in. They know how asset ownership provides cash flow, and what's enough cash flow to move on with the rest of their life.

Seeing the big picture—why and how to achieve ownership of your freedom—is what we refer to as "principles before strategy, and strategy before tactics." It's about knowing what you want and then making a plan, not the other way around. This trips up a lot of people if not properly understood. The wrong tactics, or a strategy that doesn't stem from a foundational principle, can waste a lot of time and energy. That's why it's our Principle #4.

CHAPTER 7

THE MIND OF MONEY

BY DAN S. KENNEDY

have in my office, received as a thank-you gift, an *actual* Money Tree. All its leaves are $20 bills. It reminds, of course, of the usually irritated warning from our fathers or grandfathers that "money *doesn't* grow on trees" – meaning: getting money is difficult, not simple; hard, hard, hard, not easy. While it IS technically accurate that money *in the form of money* doesn't grow on trees, it does in the form of valuable, harvestable, saleable produce and in the form of valuable timber. The Christmas tree sold at the corner lot by the gas station in your town is a money tree, for its grower and its seller. But more importantly, it is very much incorrect that money is mysteriously complicated or necessarily difficult and hard to come by, and such "programming" can and does get in the way, between people and money. I keep the tree with the leaves of $20 bills around to remind me of *that*.

The good news is that Money has rules it lives by. If you will take the trouble to know those rules, you can find it relatively simple and easy to attract Money. If you fail to learn the rules Money lives by and try to attract it while acting in conflict with it, you will find it a never-ending struggle. (If you do struggle, despite having a great formal education, high-level skills, providing meritorious service, etc., this is the likely reason: basic, fundamental conflict with Money and the rules it lives by.)

The other news, to many people, the *amazing* news is that Money has a mind of its own. It makes *independent* decisions about where to go and where not to go or to exit, who to favor and who to snub. This means its movements are PREDICTABLE. If you take the trouble to learn its reasoning and basis for these decisions, you can place yourself in the flow of money and can rather easily attract it.

If this sounds "airy-fairy," *it isn't.* I'm just about the least airy-fairy guy you could ever meet. My overriding philosophy is pragmatism. You CAN go six steps too far with this, into "magic," like the most extreme metaphysical ideas of "manifestation." I'll say: sorry, but I don't care how ardently you desire and vividly imagine a new Lambo while you sit beneath the oak tree, one will not drive itself up and toss you its keys. Money is *not* magical. Money is probably the most consistently, constantly rational actor you could ever encounter.

I have written an entire book about what I call "pragmatic and practical metaphysics": *No B.S. Wealth Attraction In The New Economy.* It describes twenty-eight Wealth Magnets, some having to do with what and how you think about wealth, others about what you do; about behavior, to attract wealth. Both sets of magnets are mission-critical. Here, I'm going to zero in on two attraction strategies well-synced with the target of Financial Freedom, as prescribed by Dr. Phelps.

Warning: For Its Reasons, Money Moves On and Leaves People Behind

One other point, a warning, one you probably won't like but please hear me out. There is enormous hazard in developing, even mastering and perfecting a single, narrow skill-set.

I had an interesting childhood experience I call: Rich Dad, Poor Dad, Same Dad. I'll try not to bore you with too much grainy detail, but the story is important and, I promise, directly relevant to you. For a time, when I was a kid, our family had a very high income from my father's small business, a commercial art studio, employing four full-time people plus part-timers, all housed in the basement of our very large home, generating from $50,000 to $100,000 a year net in the 1960s. Do the math! This kind of business existed inside the advertising industry. It "set type," for some years by manual equipment, then the first "tech wave" of phototypesetting, and it put the set type, photos, and graphics together as printer-ready "originals" for print ads, brochures, catalogs, and newsletters. The skill-sets were as a "type-setter" and as a "lay-out artist," working on a drawing board with an X-Acto Knife and rubber cement. At these two skill-sets, my father was a "master." Then came the second wave of tech, much more sophisticated phototypesetting equipment that virtually eliminated 75 percent of the skill needed and generated 90 percent finished work itself. It was then extraordinarily expensive, and after considerable angst, my parents decided not to go into debt and buy this new technology.

The business's downhill slide began shortly thereafter. In the long term, the alternate decision would only have prolonged the inevitable, because computers, particularly the earliest Apple, killed the entire typesetting and commercial art industry as it had existed. Quickly, one relatively low-skilled person and a desktop computer could replace hundreds of thousands of dollars of equipment and a half dozen fairly high-paid humans. In this way, the two skill-sets fell from high value to low value to no value at rocket speed. And also at shocking speed, we were a poor family, and I do mean *poor*.

The two skill-sets fell from high value to low value to no value at rocket speed.

My father was a very intelligent, very capable, multi-talented man who got stuck inside a single, narrow skill-set. The setback was so great he never really recovered. Make no mistake, I am NOT faulting the decision made not to invest in the high-tech makeover of the business. The major mistakes here were in not evolving in the manner described in chapter ten, in not broadening the skill-set(s) to be more adaptable and moveable, agile, and anti-fragile. By this, he wound up in a place impossible to attract Money to. Money was done with that place. It moved on and was not waiting for or returning to aid even the most virtuous who fell behind.

In contrast – not claiming utter genius, but in part directed by my observation and experience – I started in the same advertising industry, and I started with those same two skill-sets, but I quickly moved to the "creative" aspects of advertising; positioning strategy, copywriting, and media selection. These skill-sets are infinitely harder to obsolete, are much more valuable (because they are more directly tied to the selling of things), and, maybe most importantly, are very moveable. Neither new media nor new tech de-values these skills. As a result, I have been able to enjoy an uninterrupted, never threatened, high-income professional practice for 45-plus years. I also, however, moved myself through the evolution in chapter 3, so that, when medical calamity stopped my personal production, finances were not a crisis atop the other crisis. Looking back, there is no doubt in my mind that my father was more than capable of developing these same, far less fragile skill-sets and integrating them with the original business so that, while it would have to itself evolve and change, it would never have been destroyed. Further, he certainly could have moved through chapter 3's evolution faster during the Rich Years. I don't mean this as harsh critique; more as rueful regret. His suffering was not necessary. He could have always been in places where Money could and would come when called. Of course, what someone doesn't know, someone just doesn't know. But now YOU do.

My parents were great readers and consumers of "success literature," self-improvement books, and audio programs, and I consumed all they did and more. I benefited in many ways, and I am grateful for being shown that "world" from an early age. I will say, however, that all these books and recordings leaned philosophical and theoretical, focusing on principles but never connecting them to strategies, and never connecting strategies to tactics. Very heavy on what to think; light on what to do. When I entered this field, I made a point to be pragmatic, not just philosophical. Not just operating at 10,000 feet above the earth but also sleeves rolled up, hands dug into the earth. I suspect, had the material being consumed by my parents been as balanced, and been more blunt, candid, and straightforward about what needs done, not just what needs thought, different results would have occurred. I have never said that anywhere else in print or from the stage in my entire career, but found it coming out here and now, for whatever reason.

This is why I often criticize, as a symbol of all this, the famous "firewalk" gimmick of the personal growth seminars. Unless you intend to be a professional firewalker, magician, or stunt man, after its momentary excitement ebbs, now what? What do you DO?

Money *constantly* leaves and moves on – often surprising a lot of people, particularly those "caught" with highly developed, narrowly focused technical skills thought of as a lifetime warranty of invulnerability. It's only a few years ago that, in a discussion with a client of mine who leads a large, national group of orthodontists, I said that he and his field seemed safe from "being Amazon-ed" the way, say, lawyers were being chewed at by LegalZoom.com; after all, who is going to buy do-it-yourself orthodontics? And boy was I wrong. As you very well know, Smile Direct Club has begun the crash of fees and profits from braces and Invisalign®.

There has been a decade or so long "boom" in demand and income for what I affectionately call "computer geeks," notably coders and programmers. Hillary Clinton and Joe Biden have even suggested we re-train all the coal miners as programmers. This occupation category feels a lot like typesetters to me. I think 90 percent will be as extinct as dinosaurs, at a sudden, dramatically increasing pace, as the computers code and program themselves. I can't claim to be a coding or programming "expert," but I have seen this movie before. ALL "hard" skills, ALL technical (and clinical) skills are threatened in much the same way. It's the "soft," broadly applicable or mobile and moveable that suffer the least peril. The urgency to move through chapter 3's evolution is rarely clearly, blatantly visible. There's no Paul Revere riding around waking everybody up, yelling "the collapse of your skills' value is coming," and if there is, most people will ignore him. **It's up to *you* to grasp your own vulnerability and its urgency.**

It is very easy to be a today version of my Rich Dad, suddenly Poor Dad. I promise you, the fragility is there even if you can't see it (or choose not to see it) and don't feel it, and it is likely more urgent than you can know. Creating "anti-fragility" needs priority.

The most anti-fragile, the most adaptable, the most moveable skill-set I know of is management of The Business of Your Money. It is also, from a security and freedom standpoint, the most essential.

So, the final secret here about the mind of Money is: Money abhors weakness. It rarely flows to the weak, and never stays with the weak; whether weak-minded or weak, i.e., fragile and vulnerable. You and I move money to the weak, via taxes paid to the government that redistributes the proceeds and by our voluntary charity. But Money free to do as it chooses gravitates to strength. The less fragile you make yourself, intellectually, emotionally, and practically, the more comfortable Money is coming your way. When it is said that "the rich get richer and the poor get poorer," this is the mostly misunderstood truth behind the statement. For this reason, making yourself strong in every respect is the only real way to make yourself safe.

Bonus, Reprinted From *The Dan Kennedy Wealth Report* Exclusively For Freedom Founders

HOW <u>NOT</u> TO TALK TO MONEY
(Warning: It IS Listening)

The king called in the realm's most famous psychics and prophets to tell him about his future. The first predicted that all the king's friends and staunchest allies would die before he did, leaving him to live his end years alone and lonely. That prophet was promptly beheaded. The next prophet more wisely predicted that the king would outlive all his enemies. That prophet was rewarded with treasure. Point being, it matters *how* we say things, even the same things.

You may think about money as an inanimate object, but it has energy. You may not realize it, but you speak to it a lot. And how you speak to it has consequences. **What you think to yourself about money is what you say to your powerful subconscious "system"** encompassing magnetic attraction, intuition, judgment, focus, and more. It takes your thoughts about money as *directions to implement*. What you say about money to yourself and in "idle" conversations with others is heard as *"your wish is my command"* by this system. Repetition reinforces the directions. This is why "casual" affirmations like "day late and a dollar short, that's me" are so harmful. It doesn't even matter if that has been accurate up until now; where could the benefit possibly be in reinforcing it as your present and future?

DO YOU HAVE "THE YIPS?" Golfers get the yips under the pressure of "big" putts. When I did a lot of in-trenches, one-on-one work with chiropractors on case presentations and pre-pay/cash practice situations, I found the docs would get the yips when it came time to make the big putt; present the fee and the terms. *The cause of a "no" response was rarely the patient reacting to the fee or terms; it was the patient reacting to the doc's yips.* His discomfort with it telegraphed discomfort to the patient. This is the doc's *discomfort with money* oozing out. It's called "transference of thought/feeling." A perfectly calm horse becomes a nervous horse with nervous hands on the reigns. I began my deep study of "transference of thought" with a book about it from 1936, by Edmund Shaftsbury. This plays in financial negotiations of every stripe: selling, buying. At the time (in the late 1970s – early 1980s) we were charging doctors $30,000 a year for "practice management coaching." A "secret" was more of the successful results were due to working on the doctors' inner games than their outer games, specifically, working on ending their yips about money.

CHAPTER 8

PRINCIPLE № 4:

PRINCIPLES BEFORE STRATEGIES, STRATEGIES BEFORE TACTICS

BY DR. DAVID PHELPS

"There are no victims, only volunteers."

Lee Milteer

he tactics and strategies you adopt for your business and wealth must be designed to achieve a goal, such as owning your freedom. Don't put the cart before the horse by employing tactics and strategies without a clearly defined goal with objectives stated.

FREEDOM QUESTIONS:

....

Do you have an overarching plan for your assets? Are they working in concert to generate cash flow? How are the tactics you deploy helping you own your freedom? Do you have any dead or under-deployed equity? Are your assets working for you as hard as they should be? Are you positioned to mitigate the risk of an economic downturn or recession? Do you know how to hedge and position for up and down markets?

I recently had a blueprint day with Dr. Sydney and her husband Dave, who's the practice's office manager and marketing lead. His background is in copywriting and administration, which means his skills perfectly complement Dr. Sydney's technical expertise. In their late fifties, the two make for an accomplished power couple. Their solo practice is going on thirty years.

Based in the Pacific Northwest, Sydney and Dave are outdoors people. They love kiteboarding, hiking together, and being physically fit.

The reason they reached out to me was because they, like so many, crave more freedom. Could they put the business aside, call it a good run, and go have fun while they still had their health? Like many people, they were uncertain.

The couple's particular type of uncertainty was they had a handful of assets but little understanding of how they should be using them. There was no synergy, no plan. They had value in her business, good assets in stocks, bonds, mutual funds, some in retirement accounts, and a few real estate holdings—single-family homes that weren't producing great cash flow and were becoming too management intensive.

The big uncertainty: *With these existing assets, how close were they to owning their freedom?*

It didn't take us long to find some areas of improvement that could quickly get them to owning their freedom.

The main standout item: they had an office building free and clear, and other real estate free and clear, but it wasn't *working* for them. It was *dead equity*, sitting there when it could be generating revenue if they put it to use. Oftentimes, this "under-deployed equity" can be optimized to generate cash flow—perhaps even enough cash flow to eventually replace active income.

> ## Under-deployed equity can be optimized to generate cash flow— perhaps even enough cash flow to eventually replace active income.

Optimized Equity

There's often a disconnect—we want cash flow but we don't use the equity we have. That's because optimizing equity sometimes means going back into debt. For example, many of us pay off a building and feel great to be free and clear. No more debt! It's the Dave Ramsey-esque approach of paying off all debt. Sure, it can make you feel good, but it also creates dead equity.

If you have equity but it's not giving you what you want—like freedom in your lifestyle, freedom to pull the plug on trading hours for dollars—then your equity may be under-deployed.

Take an accounting of the assets and ask, "Are these working for me as hard as they should be? Are all my assets optimized?"

You can leave equity alone if you have enough cash flow. If you don't, then perhaps the equity could generate the cash flow you need.

An under-optimized asset could likewise be a business that's taking too much of your time, not producing the net profit that it could. So, what if you sold the business, took that equity, and moved it to something else that took less of your time and produced more of a regular cash flow? These are questions we explore with couples like Sydney and Dave.

During the blueprint day, we determined that Sydney and Dave lacked a strategy based on ownership and equity geometry—the assets they had weren't working ideally and they took too much of their free time to manage (this is a very common theme for the hardworking professionals in Freedom Founders). By *optimizing* their assets, the couple could quickly see a path to doing more of what they liked. Soon enough, they could own their freedom.

The key is to optimize equity enough so that it provides for the owner's specific goals in their timeline. If you know your goals, then you can determine if it's producing enough, if it's taking too much time, or if a particular investment might become vulnerable to a market shift.

Tactics follow the strategy. Tactically, to optimize Sydney and Dave's equity, we had a few options. Do we sell? Do we exchange? Do we refinance and pull money out? The different tactics depend on one's personal situation, so we looked at all their numbers on paper. We wanted Sydney and Dave to see whether or not they had the assets in total that could be optimized and then tactically used to produce better income. To show that if we do all that, could we meet their Freedom Number plus the "safe harbor" 20 percent?

In this instance, we calculated that if they sold the practice, they'd still have a gap of $500,000. So we went back to the assets, asking: Is there something else we need to do with those assets? Does Sydney need to optimize the number one asset in this case, which is her practice? Could she optimize it by ramping up the income, bringing on an associate to get her to that additional equity piece that she needs then to meet her freedom?

When we went through the puzzle of looking at all of the accounting of Sydney and Dave's assets, we found they had over $3.2 million, most of which needed to be reallocated and optimized. They saw that if we optimized it they could live on a conservative 10 percent yield or return on investments alone, without needing to draw from their investments.

The Freedom Blueprint gave Sydney and Dave the confidence to say, "We can go ahead and put the business on the market for sale now and not wait a year, two years, three years, five years, or indefinitely like so many people."

As of this writing, Sydney and Dave have been part of our group for only six months. With their blueprint in hand, the practice is now up for sale. They feel confident. They feel good. You can see the stress is gone—relief on their faces whenever we talk virtually or engage at our live Freedom Founders member meetings. They see the future. More kiteboarding and hiking. More freedom. It's not a "someday" dream, but a reality right in front of them.

In this chapter, we cover how to do what we did for Sydney and Dave. Start with big picture goals and guidelines, use those to land on a strategy, then run with a few tactics to execute the strategy and achieve the goals.

Principles, Strategies, and Tactics

Principles

These are the big rules. Your code of conduct. Your non-negotiables. The guardrails in your life that keep you on track and which you'll never cross. These inform how you behave and can encompass your values. Your principles generally don't change. They are foundational to who you are. Those who have proven to be successful in life, in spite of challenges and setbacks, are those who have a list of governing principles for almost everything. They become the filter through which major decisions are made.

For example, your household principle might be financial autonomy and freedom: "We affirm we want to have as much control, knowledge, and understanding of our investments as possible." This is in contrast to those who say, "Investment is too complicated, so I'll hire a fund manager."

Strategies

Strategies make the principal practical and actionable. These are what connect your principles to the daily tactics you execute. Strategies comprise your overarching plan or set of goals. Your strategy can (and should) change, depending on economic and market conditions.

For example: "I can redeploy monies from my 401(k) into self-directed accounts or real estate investments and reduce the potential losses from stock market volatility. I can harvest equity from assets that are not working for me at all. I can exchange current equity in low cash-flow producing properties that are creating too much time and headache from management."

Tactics

Lastly, these are the specific actions or steps taken to accomplish your strategy. Tactics come and go. You use them when you need them. Don't get attached, as the best tactic today might be the worst tomorrow.

For example: "Based on advice and data from my mentor, I've decided to invest more in equity/ownership investments for more asset growth and inflation hedging." Or, "I want to move my capital to debt assets for safety and the ability to pivot those funds after a market correction."

We cover principles, strategies, and tactics in this order because too often we do the opposite. We put tactics first, then, when we're not reaching our goals, we're confused. *I'm working so hard—shouldn't I be closer?*

For example, putting a tactic first usually sounds like "There's a really 'good deal' available for investment (can you say, "bitcoin"?)—I should grab it because someone said it was good." Good, relative to what?

Principles provide the filter for quickly determining appropriate strategy, which then determines the tactics.

Avoid the Shotgun Approach

What I often see is people start with tactics. We like to chase the bright shiny object! The deal of the day, or whatever we need in business to put out the current fire. "I need more clients, so let's get an SEO hire or a direct mailer." In investing, it's chasing that day's most profitable buy or what's making headlines—but doing so means you're late in the game.

Turn it around. First, start with principles, which set a foundation allowing you to filter the right strategies from the wrong. I start with what I want my life and time to look like—my freedom, options, and choices, i.e., what's really important to me and my family. Is it quantity of life, quality, or some mix in-between? If I venture out and build a life based on society's definition of success or based on the "successful business owner avatar in my industry," *who else* is paying a price for my un-principled and poorly defined goal?

Do I take on debt or reduce debt? Do I want more control of my investments (time and activity), or do I want more freedom and less control? These are principles. They must be defined first and foremost.

In Freedom Founders, the tactics we use are specific to investments that we make by design and intention. When a member first sees all the different possible investments, it's like a kid in a candy store—I don't know what to choose! The question is: what's right for me?

We determine what's right with strategy. The strategy for each member is based on their Freedom Blueprint and the foundational principles that are defined. That's where we customize strategies. Then based on those, we arrive at the different tactics.

The whole goal is to gain freedom and autonomy as early in life as possible. The strategies build on where you are, your values, the assets you have. Then we roll with the tactics. It shouldn't be done backward, but that's how so many do it! This is certainly common in the traditional retirement planning models that are based on saving and possibly "retiring" somewhere in the 60-70 age bracket, again, with no certainty or mile markers to measure the progress.

If you put tactics first, then you'll find that sometimes your assets work at cross purposes. Many times I review a member's financial plans and find a hodge-podge of non-correlated financial products with no plan at all. Sometimes, they spin out of control and become a huge time sink. And sometimes, your assets become liabilities that cost hundreds of thousands of dollars—that's the case with Doug Davidson in the next story.

Whatever the case, no matter how bad you think it is, there's always hope. The key to finding the light at the end of the dark tunnel is a plan that starts with principles before strategies, strategies before tactics. That's how you can optimize what you own (your assets) to ensure you reach your freedom goals sooner, not "someday."

Learning the Hard Way: Dr. Doug Davidson

Dr. Doug Davidson, 41, has been practicing dentistry for about fifteen years. He got started out of school very quickly under the guidance of a really strong mentor in dentistry. Then he was given the opportunity to buy into that practice.

In speaking with Doug at his blueprint day in 2020, he spoke with a lot of thankfulness about how his mentor taught him the business side and relationship side of a practice. Doug learned firsthand how to be a good business steward and a strong, ethical worker. Doug also has a gift for communication with patients that only flourished under the mentor's tutelage. You couldn't ask for a better way to jumpstart a young professional's career.

With his many gifts, Doug applied himself to a number of ventures over the years. But when we started looking at how his assets were contributing to his freedom, we quickly noticed a pattern—or a lack of one. His assets had no rhyme or reason. They were spread out like scatter-shot, all over the place. Textbook shotgun approach.

> ## His assets had no rhyme or reason. They were spread out like scattershot, all over the place.

Because Doug didn't have a set of principles and guidelines to use in investing outside of his practice, he was doing all kinds of things. He had put money in with some other practice owners who went together into real estate. While those assets haven't lost a lot of money, he also hasn't made any. Then he lost money in another venture, where he financed mobile vans that allow dentists to practice at nursing homes—a good idea that failed in execution.

At the same time, Doug owned a part-interest in a tugboat company working on the Gulf. "He puts these tugboats to work," said Doug of the operator. "He's really good and he makes a lot of money.

"That's great," I said. "I get it. But, Doug, how much *control* do you have over this investment? How much due diligence did you do?

"Well, I didn't. When I need to get a K-1 for the end of the year, to show whatever income or losses we had for taxes, it took me like five calls to get it."

The tugboat operator is such a small business that Doug has no control over it. By selling this investment, Doug would have more time—and money—to invest in a venture aligned with his principles and strategies.

Another thing he did is not uncommon to young professionals when they're still in school. What happens is "financial advisors" seek out young students who don't know any better to sell them on financial services that are mostly insurance-based under the guise of also being an investment in a different package.

The insurance salespeople will come to the schools before these kids even graduate and sell them into whole life insurance policies, which are heavy on the commissions on the front end and very low on the coverage until way down the road. Fresh out of school, Doug got locked into a long-term contract where he's having to pay about $36,000 a year, with another ten years to pay into it. After that point, he will have paid $400,000 in premiums for a cash value death benefit worth a million dollars.

Any unbiased mentor would tell a young professional that whole life insurance is not a prudent investment, especially for one who has so much opportunity in business and real equity assets as investment—instead, *term* life insurance is most always the cheapest and best way to go.

Imagine if Doug had invested $400,000 in an asset aligned with his principles. He'd be doing way better than just sinking the money into a life insurance policy. (Benefitting from that sort of alignment early in your life is something I, too, learned the hard way.)

Imagine if Doug had invested $400,000 in an asset aligned with his principles.

On top of all that, Doug invested in two nearby rental properties, both of which were destroyed by a recent thousand-year flood. Because he had no flood insurance for the properties, he lost the entire investment. All told, Doug has lost about $1 million.

Losing that amount would crush most anyone. But Doug is a go-getter, a survivor. Even better, he has learned a lot from these experiences. And, he's still relatively young.

Today, Doug would be the first to admit that he didn't have any overarching principles guiding his asset acquisitions. He just bought what he could when opportunities surfaced. This approach is where many of us start. It can be enough of an all-consuming endeavor just to build equity and acquire assets in the first place! I always applaud anyone who has *something*, because taking some kind of action is better than taking none at all.

"Dr. Davidson," I said, when we first spoke, "you have all these gifts and you're a go-getter. What we need to do is *focus* your energy—develop an overall philosophy. We need the right big-picture plan. You have all of the characteristics necessary to do this. You've got the work ethic. You've got the business, which is the engine. But now, instead of scatter-shooting all of these investments, we need to focus on the goal of creating cash-flow replacement for your active income."

We started with no principles or strategy. By the end of our meeting, he had both, and a new plan that ensured his tactics would help him win the war, not just a battle or two.

Doug's strategy became to acquire specific assets based on his time, risk tolerance, and desire for growth and income. The tactics helped us turn a young man who wants to invest but doesn't know how into an investor who knows what his assets are doing for him.

Once we got all that straightened out and had a goal in mind, his path to freedom became clear. Before the blueprint day finished, I said, "You've got to resist these other bright, shiny objects. They're always going to be out there for a guy like you who's so well connected."

"I'm on it," Doug said. "No more tugboats."

My Own Story: From Shotgun to Sustainability

While I was initially strategic in focusing on real estate early in my career, I likewise started with no overriding principles. Had I had any sort of philosophy or guidelines, I could have done well far sooner. Why didn't I have a philosophy?

The biggest reason was I started with no mentors. As a young person, I didn't know what I didn't know about mentors, collaboration, and networking relationships. I hadn't read any books about philosophy or principles. Like most, I was stuck on strategy and a lot of tactics.

As soon as I pursued association and found some good mentors, I began developing my own personal philosophy. Rather than learn one specific way of doing things—one career, one technical skill, one standard in an industry or profession—I started believing in the idea that other ways could offer more. I ascertained that there were many roads to Dublin (freedom) and that I owed it to myself and my family to explore some of those paths.

It worked. Had I had the advantage of having a mentor or somehow discovered on my own by reading books and developed this multi-path philosophy earlier, I might have created my freedom that much faster. But better late than never.

The journey, though, wasn't easy. The strategies and tactics I started with cost me time and money as I learned through trial and error. For example, I started with single-family houses, which could have been an overarching principle—gaining freedom on smaller deals of single-family rather than commercial. But soon I deviated by doing other ventures in real estate. These weren't necessarily failures, but they did take me off point because they were new and I spent so much time learning about them. Once my eye was off the ball, I started thinking about a dozen different ventures and assets. I got involved in commercial real estate, real estate notes, mobile home park communities, and more. Could these work? Maybe. Were they the fastest way to get me closer toward my goal? Probably not.

Deviating may seem fun or exciting, but sometimes we need a reality check. Deviating can delay your freedom. I went on a tangent, out of my lane for a time, until I realized that those things were distracting from my speed.

Deviating can delay your freedom.

Then came a moment when I urgently realized I needed to prioritize principles—I couldn't just aggregate a plethora of disparate tactics forever. That happened when Jenna was in the hospital recovering from her liver transplant. It didn't take me long to realize I couldn't waste any more time.

In considering selling my practice, relying on the cash flow from real estate, and spending as much time as I could with my family, I went deep into thought about how to coordinate my assets to reach these goals.

I thought: *What do I have? What are my assets? What are they producing right now? And if I'm going to pull back and stop my active income, then how do I make these assets produce enough income that still provides for my family? I can't be experimenting around now, so with my skill sets, knowledge base, and assets, what's the best way to continue producing income sustainably?*

Making your "active income" your overall philosophy can only get you so far. Sure, the best part of active income is its sustainability—as long as you're able to do the transactional work. Active income can fill in gaps, make up for mistakes. Like Doug Davidson—at 41 years old, the world is not over for him. As long as he's healthy, he can get up to bat again. But it's when we get older in life or when we lose the ability to produce active income that we can't afford to become distracted. That's when we must have more robust guiding principles. You'll see that and more in each of the three avatars ahead.

The Three Avatars—Which One Are You?

1. The Young Gun

Stephen Covey says in his book, *The 7 Habits of Highly Effective People*, "Begin with the end in mind." Well, a young person doesn't know where the end is because they're at the beginning, while the end is too far beyond the horizon. Much of what's ahead is foggy. The Young Gun may want to start building a life, a family, and a business, buy a better house, and level up on cars and vacations. It's fun to think about all the possibilities!

But in all the excitement, what ends up happening is the young business owner focuses solely on tactics. It's a lot of "do, do, do," with no principles to guide him or her and leverage their efforts towards ownership and freedom. At this point in their career, they have no milestones, no metrics to measure anything. Nothing's been set yet. It's all so new. That's at least how it was for me.

This period can go on for a while unless you find a mentor. Mentors are key. Being an "apprentice" under the guidance of someone else for at least a few years pays huge dividends down the road because you actually get to see through the eyes of somebody else what constructs work—what's important to be thinking about in life.

At the same time, you're building relationships you can rely on. These are relationships with a spouse, with close friends and family, with associations. These are the people who can help you make decisions and pursue the path toward freedom. You're building these relationships anyway in life, so might as well make sure at the same time that you're also on the same page with others as you form goals and guidelines.

Bottom line: *Get a mentor. Join a few groups (where you're not the smartest person in the room). Align your relationships with your goals.*

2. The Mid-Career Maverick

By mid-career, we're usually consumed by many responsibilities. To our family, to our kids of different ages and needs. To our career, which is in the midst of our highest-earning years, from forty to fifty-five years old.

As a Mid-Career Maverick, you're spread out. If you feel that way, it may be because you haven't landed on your set of guiding principles. You may need a different strategy—but which one?

Do you expand the business? Start a new venture? Join an exciting opportunity? It's tough to know the right strategy without first having the overriding principles to guide you.

To paraphrase mom: Avoid doing something just because it's right for somebody else. Just copying somebody else's strategy because they're doing it is a recipe for a big headache, or worse.

In your profession, are you taking extra courses or bringing on a new technology? Serving a new clientele? Specializing in a niche? Building or expanding to bigger just because you can and it makes you feel successful?

Mid-career is the time when you are likely tossing around a lot of different strategies and tactics. But keep in mind that strategies and tactics aren't fruitful just because they're new or different from what you've been doing. They may add a little fuel to the fire and some momentum but in the bigger scheme of things, they don't necessarily translate to any more freedom.

Start defining your freedom: *What's your definition of "Doing what I want, with whom I want to do it, where I want to do it, how I want to do it, and whenever I want"?*

Design your principles around that definition, then target strategies best related to you and your goal. What are your traits? What is your personality? What are your skills, assets, and associations? These inform your strategies too.

Then put blinders on and figure out what tactics best match your goals. Figure out where you fit and those who you need to surround yourself with to build your path to freedom following your principles.

3. The End-Career Sage

If you're at the end of your career, ready for what's next, yet you're:

    a.   Uncertain about when exactly you can call it quits, or

    b.   Skeptical you'll ever have *enough,*

then it's likely your strategies, tactics, or principles are unaligned or lacking. That's okay! Remember, it's never too late.

If we consider Maslow's hierarchy of needs, you may have taken care of most needs on the pyramid. But what about purpose, significance, and meaning? Oftentimes, at the end of our careers, we're still searching for purpose and meaning. These are within reach, yet just may require ending one career and beginning anew in something else.

To gain some certainty about *when* you can transition, we take a stark look at your investment base. We're asking the big question: *How can your assets last you the rest of your life?*

In Freedom Founders, we talk about the Freedom Number and having enough assets to produce regular cash flow. So knowing the financial side—the principles for sustainable cash flow and asset preservation—is one piece of the puzzle.

The other side is more existential: *"Who am I now? What am I going to be when I leave the business? What are the principles that will help guide me to who that person is going to be? What does that version of me do? How do I act? Where do I give back? Where do I spend my time? How do I still remain fruitful and relevant to society? How do I still feel good about myself, my family, and my spouse?*

I recently had a blueprint day for a couple in this very position. Empty-nesters both in their sixties, they work together in the business. They feel dragged down by the day-to-day operations and ready to move on—but to what? The big question was, "What do I do next?" (My book *What's Your Next?: The Blueprint for Creating Your Freedom Lifestyle* helps you answer these very questions.)

As an end-career sage, now is the perfect time to dig down deep inside and do some inner work. It's never too late to dig in and find your principles.

Free for Life™

Free for Life™ is the moment you realize your aligned principles, strategies, and tactics have worked for you. After working with many of our members to put principles before strategies and strategies before tactics, I'm always thrilled when I get a call or see them in a meeting, and I can tell they're glowing. Pure relief and joy. They've done it! They put in the hard work, got smart about aligning it, and now are floating on joy.

Free for Life™ is the moment you realize your aligned principles, strategies, and tactics have worked for you.

It's one of those moments like walking across the graduation stage for a degree. You've been working all the time to get to that top of the pinnacle. And, finally, you've achieved it. You're recognized for it. It's solidified. Certified. You're Free for Life™.

Free for Life™ isn't retirement. It's not, "go play golf five days a week." It's not even an end. Rather, it's a new reality, a new phase when life for you starts to expand. You're owning your freedom, with the options and choices in life not to do nothing but to do what you really want.

Several years ago, I had one couple in for a blueprint day, and, on the spot, after running the numbers, we determined they were already Free for Life™. They hadn't even sold the practice, but with their combination of assets they were Free for Life™ whether they sold it or not. In other words, his comment was, "I can throw the keys to the office in the bushes!"

Now, we're not talking about walking away entirely (they did end up selling it). But it gave them huge relief to know the asset wasn't even critical to their freedom. Most people think if you have a business, you've got to sell it. Well, maybe. You definitely *want* to sell the business, simply because it has some market value. And because it was your baby all those years, you want to see it taken care of. But imagine that it's *not* a critical piece of your freedom. Imagine *not* being boxed into a corner. Imagine not having to sell it for a premium because you aren't sure you have enough—the uncertainty conundrum strikes again!

Another member couple, Dr. Mike Dostal and his dentist spouse, Lauren, are not yet forty years old, have young children at home, and have hit their Freedom Number. Yet Mike's not ready to hang it up and play golf six days a week. No way! He loves being in a position of freedom and choices and designing his participation in his practices (they have two) in such a way that he can do the procedures and see the patients he wants to see on *his* schedule—not because he has to be all things to all people on a five day work week predicated by insurance dictates.

Mike's latest plans are adding additional associates, dropping another clinical day per week (from three days to two), and taking two years off with Lauren starting in 2027 to be *international students* along with their children. *This* is freedom!

Sometimes, the only thing in our way is a little imagination, clarity of purpose, and the security of knowing when enough is enough.

Chances are, you're closer than you think!
Visit www.OwnYourFreedomBook.com/Resources
to experience the incredible stories of Free for Life™
members and the impact it has had on their lives.

CHAPTER 9

WHO'S GOING TO DRIVE YOUR CAR?

BY DAN S. KENNEDY

How To Arrive At FREEDOM, On Time, Without Any Wrong Turns!

I have several topics here:

- ★ Delegation vs. Abdication
- ★ Information vs. Opinion
- ★ Right vs. Right *For You*
- ★ Billy Joel's Caution

Let's start with Delegation vs. Abdication.

No matter how well paid by fees, commissions, or other incentives; no matter how honest and ethical; no matter how expert, who is MOST likely to be MOST concerned, MOST consistently, with the achievement of *your* goals with *your* money? – a "hired gun" or you?

This is a simple question that many people would prefer NOT considering and that the giant "financial services industry" hopes you never ponder!

If, however, you are going to do anything more than bury cash in coffee cans in your backyard like Grandpa or Tony on *The Sopranos*, you are going to have no alternative but to involve other people, 2nd parties, and 3rd parties with your money. As a control freak and DIY'er, I don't *like* this, but a mentor taught me to be careful not to let my small likes 'n dislikes get in the way of the big achievements and results I want most. He said that he imagined birds would like to sleep in and disliked getting up before dawn, especially on chilly, rainy days, but since there were no worms left after 8:00 A.M. and they wanted to eat, up 'n at 'em. For success at anything, you have to learn to manage yourself and to manage others, carefully chosen.

Jay Van Andel, co-founder of Amway, had a speech he frequently gave titled *DELEGATE OR STAGNATE.* He was right. But far too many people, including far too many business or practice owners, DON'T delegate within The Business of Their Money. Instead, they ABDICATE. That means: (a) FAILURE to fulfill one's duty or responsibility; (b) surrendering one's throne. In practical terms, it means surrender of control *by* surrender of responsibility, so that you are wholly dependent on the judgment and faithful performance of others, in managing The Business of Your Money. From the opportunity to be King to the reality of being (hopefully) taken care of by other kings.

There are all sorts of excuses that sound like good reasons for such abdication: *too busy; too old to learn new tricks; it's too confusing; it must be better to just trust professionals in this*. But ultimately, they are all hollow. With these excuses and choices, you are stepping back, away, and aside from "driving the car." In a very real way, you are choosing to be a spectator of your money, rather than being in control of it.

DELEGATION, on the other hand, is essential. Developing a "team" of competent and reliable "implementation agents" and "facilitators" – probably including a CPA, a family attorney, providers of different financial products like insurance, stocks, bonds, structured notes, real estate, etc. and advisors, coaches, and peer investors – empowers you to support and execute a plan, utilize others' specialized knowledge and experience, and have various 'moving parts' watched over on your behalf (like relevant changes in tax law), and can be set up to have opportunities brought to you that fit *your* criteria. For example, Members of Dr. Phelps's Freedom Founders have connections to an exclusive, curated network of real estate investments brought to the group for "first dibs" before being publicly offered, a form of *legal* insider trading. This erases one of the biggest problems with real estate as an investment category, especially for busy, high "chairside value" professionals: finding doable deals and diligently analyzed opportunities. I have had a similar arrangement with a long-time provider of apartments and small commercial building investments for many years, so I was able to grow a portfolio of real estate worth millions of dollars *without* ever going on the hunt for any, and *without* having to rely only on my un-expert analysis of any. **But – this is important – I had strict criteria ruling out a lot, and I'm only delegating the finding, *not* abdicating the decision-making**. Similarly, I have one financial professional particularly skilled at structured notes, and with good access to new offerings almost every month. To her, I have delegated the finding, sifting, and sorting in keeping with my pre-fixed criteria, and I have delegated the monitoring and management of early pay-offs (which often happen), regularly scheduled pay-offs, succinct reporting of yield and gains, and of cash on hand. This "division" of my Business of My Money operates, mostly, with one phone call and one set of documents' arrival per month. However – and this is important – I am only delegating what I just described, *not* abdicating decision-making.

I'M ONLY DELEGATING THE FINDING, NOT ABDICATING THE DECISION - MAKING.

As an aside, there *is* a makeable argument for (having some portion of your assets in) "money under management" with which you *do* abdicate day-to-day decision-making, but you should still be a diligent overseer, able and willing to ask questions, and maintaining firm agreement on goals. There are safeguards you must have with this – after all, all the "investors" (victims) of Bernie Madoff *thought* they had money under management. And there is Woody Allen's old lament: "I had a money manager who managed my money until there was no money left to manage."

Yes, YOU Can

To do this necessary delegation successfully, you need (only) two things: (1) to be informed and *interested*, and (2) to have encircled yourself with people effective at what is being delegated to them. There is no question that YOU CAN do this. You have learned complicated clinical (technical) skills and business management skills. You have already gone through that process. I did not attend college, by the way, and I had to get most of this by *self*-education. If I can, and I did, then you can. There are also shortcuts and safeguards, like Dr. Phelps's Freedom Founders, designed very specifically for you, the business owner. He learned largely by self-education and built his "modus operandi" from scratch, and now essentially lets other appropriately qualified owners use what he built – which provides both shortcuts and safeguards.

One caveat: do NOT overestimate your "Lone Ranger" capabilities as you grow them. The Business of Your Money is a VERY different business from the business of your practice. There's temptation to think: *because I'm smart and successful at 'x', I'll (instantly, automatically) be just as smart and successful at 'y' too.* But even the Lone Ranger had Tonto. Think about a pilot: he has a GPS, but often a co-pilot who, in part, serves as navigator; he utilizes the air traffic control system; he utilizes a ground crew. And just because he's been really successful at driving cars, <u>he does *not* jump</u> into the pilot seat of a Cessna, let alone a 747, and take off. That would *obviously* be *foolish*.

One side note: being active in managing The Business of Your Money is a good thing, psychologically and emotionally, even for your physical health, as you transition from owning your business to owning your freedom. You have been useful, productive, in charge (thus important), and experiencing accomplishment for decades. You *need* this. Deprived of it, many suddenly freed retirees quickly discover "you can only play so much golf." Some wither and die early. Others develop various problems. Others "leap invest" in a business they know little or nothing about, in order to again feel important, productive, and in charge, and suffer big losses.

Information and Opinion; Information Vs. Opinion.

Both have useful purposes, but it is financial life-or-death important, mission-critical NOT to confuse the two.

Every person who has Information to offer also has plenty of Opinions to offer. As a consultant, I worked very hard on the self-discipline of separating these two for my clients, often saying: "Here is what I *know*," then, "here is what I *think*." Not every advisor, product provider, pundit, author, etc., is so forthright, so *you* must be discerning.

As an example, here is an item from one of the newsletters I write, from December 2020. At the time, Bitcoin was trading at dizzying highs, and, if taking profits, a lot of people made a lot of money within a period of time. That is neither here nor there. The point here is to show you the differentiation between information and opinion. I have provided both. I have straightforwardly identified what I think and believe, i.e., opinion, and identified certain facts, i.e., information. You should be able to clearly see the distinctions. When you have a "source" who does this for you, that's terrific, but remember it is YOUR money, so it is YOUR responsibility to be confident you have separated what comes to you from *any* source into two buckets: one, facts and information; two, (educated/expert) opinion.

UH-OH, IF USING BITCOIN OR ITS BROTHERS

My good friend Lee Bellinger, publisher of OFF-GRID CONFIDENTIAL, called my attention to the new, added, required-by-law checkbox item on 2020 IRS tax forms: **"At any time during 2020, did you sell, receive, send, exchange or otherwise acquire *any* financial interest in *any* virtual currencies?"** If you lie (NO) and get caught, it's a prosecutable felony, as income tax evasion. If you tell the truth (YES), you have red-flagged yourself for an audit, especially if also a high-income earner, self-employed in whole or part, filing a Schedule C, claiming home office deductions. Lee also noted that Porter Stansberry is leading a pack of promoters mailing pitches for cyber-currency newsletters. I respect Stansberry, and I certainly "get" the attraction of Bitcoin and its kin, **BUT, on this, my mind is _unchanged_:** (a) I believe it is all illegal and that a sweeping federal gov't crackdown has to come; (b) I can't get past it having NO asset support, NO insurance (like FDIC), NO transparency – it is "made up," and even its creator is a secret; (c) it invites IRS scrutiny of your entire life and finances; and (d) it creates profits and "phantom profits" on which there are tax liabilities, so those using it in utilitarian ways are likely committing tax evasion/fraud without even knowing it. IRS protocols classify cryptocurrencies as a "taxable asset," *not a currency*. Thus, if you bought a crypto-coin for $10, and it became worth $100, and you spent the $100 on bubble gum, you (probably) owe capital gains or (maybe) income tax on $90. Finally, it is volatile, subject to crash overnight. If you are of the "might-have-to-run-and-hide-out-in-the-hills" mindset, owning it seems pragmatic, but it is *not* a simple decision; it carries *unmitigated* risk of loss, and it portends consequences if you *don't* ever run for the hills. Simply, the U.S. Treasury Dept. and the IRS fear it, hate it, and are automatically suspicious of anyone buying, owning, or trading in it, and that makes me itch. I do NOT claim expertise on cryptocurrency or related tax law; I am merely reporting on *my* itch.

Here's one more example, an item I wrote for *The Dan Kennedy Wealth Report* published privately, only for Members of Dr. Phelps' Freedom Founders. Just days AFTER I wrote it, Hewlett-Packard and Oracle announced relocating their corporate HQs from Silicon Valley to Houston, Texas. Anyway, if you read carefully, you will see that I have provided both information and opinion, and that I have identified which is which. A good exercise is to get two different color hi-liter pens, say Yellow for information, Blue for opinion, and mark the item up. Your brain is trained to recognize a green light as "Go" and a red light as "Stop" – it is good to train your brain to recognize "Information" and to recognize "Opinion."

MEGA-TRENDS

John Naisbitt wrote the bestselling book by that title decades ago, its premise that there are, at times, fast developing MEGA-trends that "change *everything*." Re: real estate, the emptying of major cities is, in my opinion, just such a trend. San Francisco is emptying of young people liberated from working AT Silicon Valley, discovering that the rents *fallen* to $2,000 to $4,000.00 a month for 1-bedroom apartments in a now devastated city need not be paid; they can live and work from anywhere; they need more space for home offices. New York City, same situation. I lived through Cleveland's fall from 10 biggest cities, from 1M-plus to 300,000 residents. A number of Biggest Cities are going to lose 30-plus percent of their residents, 50 percent of their small business, and many of their big corporate HQs, either NEVER to return or being recreated 10 to 20 years in the future. Also, "space," a mega-trend. Several months ago, in new home construction, I noted that the new models would feature *TWO* home office rooms. An October 17-18 Wall Street Journal contained an article about "Sanity Sheds;" the rising demand met by companies selling pricey backyard sheds fully equipped as home offices. I had a client doing this in the '90s, in N. Ca., but then, there and elsewhere it was a relatively rare luxury. Now it will be "mainstream." The "cocooning" that futurist Faith Popcorn predicted 20 years ago IS upon us. When she foresaw it is a potential generational preference, the tech to enable it was not yet here. Now it is. If you are going to literally live *in* your phone, you *ca*n "cocoon." Maybe *most* "going out" (movie theaters, sports bars, concerts, etc.) and *most* "going to the office" will be of a past life people have left behind. This will doom malls (three big mall operators are already in Ch. 11 BK) and the communities of restaurants, night-spots, etc., encircling them; and office tower clusters and the communities of restaurants, shops, etc., encircling them. Isolating in homes will make close proximity to Work or to Entertainment and Shopping a canceled consideration, 180-degree reversing the mega-trend of the past decade. WHAT <u>YOU</u> THINK about such possibilities has to translate into actions, both threat reactive and opportunistic. What Naisbitt recognized was: **MONEY MOVES IN TANDEM WITH MEGA-TRENDS.**

Now, let's talk about *the kind of* information you need. There is *foundational* <u>information</u>, like how money works, how a particular category of investment works, or about a particular industry or business category in which you are considering buying a company's stock works. This is all readily available. You also need *situational* <u>information</u>, specific to a geographic area and its (changing) demographics, if investing in real estate, or to a company if investing in its stock. Sometimes a lot of knowledge about *one* reason favoring a stock is enough, and that is situational. Just as an example, I and a number of my private clients have done nicely with our stock in Hasbro, the toy company, acquired at a particular point in time for only one reason I deeply understand: Disney. I don't know much of anything about the toy industry, but I am a very, very serious student of Disney. When news was reported of Disney extending some exclusive licenses and granting new ones to Hasbro for toys and games tied to Disney films and characters including *Frozen*, I saw Hasbro as a cheap per-share way to own more Disney. Quick research into Hasbro itself verified my optimism about the company. Then I bought in. In a few years' time, I racked up about a 25 percent gain, took my principal back out, and kept the gains in for a free ride going forward.

Many years ago, I was having lunch with a consultant to one of the big regional banks based in Phoenix, where I lived at the time. Just making conversation, I asked him if he was working on anything interesting with the bank. He answered – and probably shouldn't have – by telling me of the pending but certain to be approved new freeway loop connecting a then fairly isolated suburb with very modestly priced, middle-class homes, low-value shopping centers, and a lot of undeveloped land to the city's hub, reducing that drive time from 40 minutes stop-n-go to 10 minutes, zoom-zoom. He went on to describe the bank's "seat at the table," to finance new development for a consortium of home builders and a big mall, where X marks the spot on the map. I bought lunch and shortly thereafter bought some of that empty land as close to "X" as I could, and I partnered in buying a clump of houses, then rental properties. It took a little while, but the profit realized was, let's just say, substantial.

So, let's talk about **"source".** It really, really, really matters. Informationand legitimate expert, specialized opinion both matter. The agenda of the source, if there is one, matters.

This is why a "network" is important. The question to ask about a question about an opportunity is: *who do you know and/or who do they know with "insider" and expert knowledge about it?* – therefore likely being a good source of both information and opinion worthy of consideration. As an example, not long ago, my interest was piqued by a news item about private investors financing personal injury legal cases, and then being paid based on the final settlements. I found a couple of companies in the business of "packaging" such investments, got their information, and remained intrigued. *Then I asked myself: who do I know? and who do they know, with insider and expert knowledge about this?* I happen to know one of the leading business advisors to P.I. law firms in the country, so I reached out to him, with: "give me your best 10 minutes on this – what you *know* first; your opinion of pros, cons, hazards second – and I'll swap you 10 minutes from me on any subject you like." He admitted limited direct knowledge, gave what he could, but also reached out to a client of his, a lawyer with a huge multi-state P.I. practice who used outside financing for big cases. From him, he got information and opinion brought back to me. Efficiently, without a lot of "from scratch" research on my own, I had enough to confidently make a stop or go further, no or maybe or yes decision.

THE WELL-STUFFED ROLODEX® - YOUR OWN & RENTED & BORROWED

It's an outdated term, but I was taught early on that the "strength" of my Rolodex® was going to play a big role in my acquiring, preserving, and growing my wealth. Belonging to formal networks is a force multiplier, because of who each of the network members knows, and then who they know. In every business I've been in or investing in, I've made a point of tapping into networks, cultivating contacts and relationships for uncertain future use, and stuffing my Rolodex.

Informal **networks** are useful, meaning those you create around you or step into, where like-minded, similarly goal-oriented people share information, opinions/ideas, and experiences. One of the famous examples is the "mastermind group" of Henry Ford, Harvey Firestone, Andrew Carnegie, and Thomas Edison, reported on by author Napoleon Hill in *Think and Grow Rich* and *Laws of Success*. Their "model" has been used often since then, in industry, finance, and politics.

Belonging to organized, purposed, *formal* coaching and mastermind groups like Dr. Phelps's Freedom Founders can be a shortcut to a well-stuffed Rolodex, in its case covering every conceivable aspect of real estate investing as the foundation of passive income replacement for active, earned income. You have your Rolodex, his Rolodex, and the other Members' Rolodexes to draw on as needed. A high-quality organizer, leader, and operator of a group like this, like Dr. Phelps, does a lot of screening and disqualifying of participants and a lot of testing, verifying, and curating of information for the group. I have personally led such groups in the fields of direct marketing and information marketing (i.e., authorship, publishing, speaking, training, etc.) for more than 30 years, in part acting as "Coach To The Coaches." I know how much energy is required to do it right, and I have witnessed firsthand, time and time again, just how much of a shortcut or accelerator of success participation can be. There are damn few *legitimate* shortcuts to success, and this is one of those rarities.

Right vs. Right FOR YOU

The financial services industry, Wall Street, and government overlords have agreed upon "standards" for how your money should be invested and managed, with allocations to different asset categories and products formulaic to your age, marital status, income, occupation, total net worth, retirement horizon, and several other factors. From this come fancy pie charts and bar graphs, often in purportedly "personalized" or "customized" proposals that are really nothing of the sort. They *have to* fall within pre-determined borders of What Is Right. Somewhat ironically, Registered Investment Advisors and Fiduciaries (RIAs), supposedly the highest and "best" levels of advisors, are the most restricted in what they dare suggest or do for you because they have the most regulatory scrutiny making sure they are doing What Is Right.

MY DAY 'STRIPPED NAKED'

A couple decades back, I bought a day of consultation from a business friend who is a "financial whiz." He is a former regional bank president and a veteran of a big, big-name Wall Street investment bank, and did a lot of finance consulting with entrepreneur-owned, mid-sized companies. As he puts it, I "stripped naked financially," walked him through what I was doing with my money, and invited his opinions. He said, "Virtually every financial professional or advisor you might ask would tell you what you are doing is *not* right. You would hear that it is *not* right for someone as young as you are – meaning: too conservative, *not* right for someone earning at your high level, *not* right for someone paying the taxes you are paying, and so on. But," he went on, "I know *you,* and you have articulated *your* objectives and *your* reasoning well, and it seems to me that what you are doing IS right *for you.*" Of course, he had no agenda, no financial products to sell, no quotas to meet, no company to satisfy, not even any regulatory issues tied to this opinion. I will tell you, I felt a lot better and more sure-footed after that day.

This is NOT to say that the standards of What Is Right, portfolio allocation, asset class diversity, income-for-life products, or any of the rest of the traditional, conventional, commonly prescribed strategies are "wrong." It is fine to consider them. **But *your* task is to get to What Is Right – *FOR YOU,*** and that may very well disagree with what 70 percent, 80 percent, even 90 percent of the "money industry" would prescribe.

One big issue, which, to their credit, advisors discuss and try to factor into recommendations (albeit in a standardized, formulaic way) is "risk tolerance." There is the risk(s) you *should and shouldn't* incur, based on age, ability to replace losses from current income (or not), legacy concerns. There is also the risk you *can and can't* handle well psychologically and emotionally. Being a "nervous Nellie" day by day about paper losses, news headlines, etc., is no way to live. One of the *principles* that Dr. Phelps and I agree on about financial risk-taking and managing is that, for the most part, at point of seriousness about "locking in" financial freedom, you want **to limit risk to only**

the size and scope necessary to meet *your* financial goals. This prohibits "wild chases" of fast, fantastic gains but it tends to also prohibit sudden, dramatic, off a cliff losses. You have to decide on your enough-is-enough numbers and then have and happily stick to a strategy for achieving and protecting *them*. That principle is probably Right for most business owners reading this book, but the details of its application, as strategy and tactics, may vary quite a bit from person to person. So, again, your task is getting to What's Right – FOR YOU.

By the way, there is **NO single-sided coin**. "Hard" assets have the virtue of being "hard", but they have the negatives of being illiquid and, if real estate related, immobile. "Liquid" assets have the virtue of their liquidity, but the negatives of volatility and greater risk of loss. Within those two categories, each specific investment is also a double-sided coin. Slightly tweaking a poem, *if wealth was simple every beggar would have a gold watch at his side and every shoeless sufferer would have a horse to ride*. There is an old, now impolitic song warning men not to marry a *pretty* woman, for all the worry over other handsomer or richer men it brings. One more demonstration that the search for a single-sided coin is a fool's errand.

The last thing to remember about this is that some asset classes and some financial and investment "vehicles" have a lot of pundit-advocates, salespeople, and entire sales organizations; others have few sales representatives in the media or knocking on your door. Annuities, for example, are much, much, much more "represented" than real estate. That does *not* necessarily make annuity products good or bad, better or worse, nor does it necessarily say anything about the merits or demerits of real estate, *FOR YOU*. It mostly exists as a reality because annuity products are much easier than real estate to create, package, manage, and sell, and that there are a lot of established sales and distribution channels for them but few such channels for real estate investments. This DOES mean you have to be careful of "laziness," in letting who, in the greatest numbers, literally or figuratively, is knocking on your door govern what you pay attention to, investigate, and consider. I have more to say about this in "Chapter 5: The Criticality of Independent Thought."

The Billy Joel Principle

The Principle is from a Billy Joel song: "sooner or later you sleep in your own bed."

It has been said differently by many different people. The actor Jack Nicholson said, "What *you* think of me is none of *my* business" – and that can apply to what others think of your financial strategies in spades. It is easy to get sucked into trying to do what others judge "right," what others approve of, what "experts" advocate, even what plays well in cocktail party conversation. Nobody wants to be the only guy at the fancy dress party in a tuxedo but with *brown* shoes. But at a point – all the experts, all the peers, all the golfing buddies, everybody else is gone – the party has ended for the night, and you are at home, having to sleep in your own bed.

What You Want vs. What You've Got & What You Get

First, #1, there is your "vision" of what *you* want. What you want your finances to be, your activities to be, your lifestyle to be, your support system to be, etc. and etc. Your freedom. The clearer that Vision, the better, by the way – which is why Dr. Phelps and his wife Kandace conduct a "Blueprint Day" with each new Freedom

Founders Member. Then, next to it, **#2, is the reality of what you've got.** The current condition of your finances, activities, lifestyle, etc. And there is, **#3, what *will* be.** How the realities will stack up against the "vision" in 3 years, 5 years, 7 years. Here is the big truth about this:

Ultimately, **whatever you accept, *is*.** And it is for as long as you accept it as it is. It doesn't matter why you accept it as it is, whether you have a perfectly legitimate reason or just an excuse masquerading as one, or whether you have somehow been placed in your "what is" by others or by circumstances over which you had no control. None of that can produce any change in what is; it can only reinforce what is. Acceptance vs. your refusal to accept what is, this is *the only thing* that can possibly, ever change a negative or unsatisfactory "what is" for the better (other than a random lightning bolt of blind, dumb luck). This puts it *all* on you, which is NOT where most people want it. That may be "unfair," but that fact of unfairness, if it is fact, will NOT change your "what is" for the better.

A miserable thunderstorm coming in the day you planned a golf outing, your first break from work in many weeks, something you've looked forward to, earned, and deserved, is unfair. But its unfairness does *not* stop the thunderstorm. In that situation, you can accept the ruination of your day off or you can refuse to accept it, and quickly decide on and substitute an indoor activity you'll enjoy. This is easier with just a planned day upset by bad weather than it is with much more serious and much bigger matters, but the core truth is the same with anything and with everything: **only your refusal to accept 'what is,' and action on that refusal, can change it.** Whatever you accept, *is*.

WHATEVER YOU ACCEPT, IS.

Let's acknowledge that: that the previous two entire paragraphs you just read SUCK. They have a "personality" not even their mother could love and they're ugly and smell foul, too. However, *you* have to find a way to love them, because only their Truth can set you free.

CHAPTER 10

PRINCIPLE №5:

INVEST IN YOUR TRANSFERABLE SKILL SETS

BY DR. DAVID PHELPS

"Be who you are and say what you feel,
because those who mind don't matter
and those who matter won't mind."

Dr. Seuss

Your skills are an asset, just as essential as what you own and who you spend your time with. Specialized, technical skills can only get you so far and are vulnerable to disruption. That's why we must invest in general skills, which can help you succeed across multiple revenue streams.

FREEDOM QUESTIONS:

....

What non-technical, non-specialized skills do you have? How could you invest further in these transferable skills? Could you apply these skills to another income stream? If something happened to your business, livelihood, or ability to practice your specialized skills, could you rely on your transferable skills?

Dr. Scott Leune graduated as a dentist in 2005. Within the first year of practice, he had a traumatic back injury while playing soccer. Essentially it made him wheelchair-bound for years, during which time he couldn't do what he was trained to do—treat patients clinically with his technical expertise.

"I had two fractured vertebrae in my back. They were crushing the nerve roots going into my legs and the pain was unbearable. And when the pain got really bad, then I'd have to be in a wheelchair. And so for about a decade or so, I was in and out of that wheelchair," he said when I interviewed him for this book.

"Here I am, twenty-six, practice opens, I'm in debt. My wife's pregnant with our first child and she's got school debt. We both graduated the same day from the same school, her as a hygienist and me as a dentist. And my practice is booming. Three to four hundred new patients a month, and I'm drowning in challenges in operating a company that's growing that fast.

"This back issue made me come to the painful realization that I cannot be a dentist. I studied all this time and went into all this debt, and I just couldn't see functionally how I could do it."

Overnight, he had to shift skill sets. Thankfully, Scott had another skill set—teaching—which was an outlet for him. "I'd always done something like coach the soccer team, or work as a chemistry instructor and dental school tutor. And so I started applying my strengths in teaching.

"I got into this mindset that said, 'Every failure I have is going to give me a teachable moment. And if I can keep having teachable moments, I can become a better instructor.' And maybe that will ultimately be what I am in dentistry since I can't be a dentist."

He went from a business operator, who owned his practice but spent all his time trading hours for dollars, to a business CEO, teacher, and marketer, bringing other doctors in to do the actual work. While he might have eventually made the shift to doing less work mid-career, the injury forced him to shift skill sets much earlier than he'd ever considered before.

Then, he had an epiphany: "I'll build companies in a way that maintains my flexibility, and if I can maintain my flexibility, I can own more companies." But it wasn't easy.

"If I'm not the operator, that means I've got to become an actual leader, someone who can lead and influence a good operator to do what's right. And that's nice to read about. And that's nice to talk about. But until I was in that position, I didn't understand how hard it actually is to do something that sounds so simple. So I lost a lot of money learning those leadership lessons, but all those lessons became teaching points, and those teaching points became the foundation to our success."

Over the next decade, Dr. Scott built ten practices, selling off most for profit in the process. In the meantime, he realized his life had so much more flexibility than when he'd been practicing full time.

"It was just nice that I could go take the kids to the doctor whenever I wanted because I'm not practicing dentistry."

Fast forward to today. Scott hasn't been doing clinical dentistry for a decade. Once he made that initial shift to CEO, he decided he liked that position. And he was good at it. He now regularly launches multiple practices, in which he brings on younger doctors and mentors them. And that's just the half of it.

"I ended up building a call center company, a building, an insurance company, a marketing company, an IT company, an education company, a consulting company, and a group purchasing organization company. Some of those companies grew to be the biggest of their class in dentistry in a very short amount of time. And I did that all without raising money and with freedom of my time while building a family. We now have five children, and I'm the soccer coach, and I take them to and from school every day. And all of that means something important to me.

"Today I've sold and merged a lot of those companies. I'm now a part leader and influencer of our organization, which doesn't take up a lot of my time but is an extremely important role. I'm part educator still, and that takes up my time. But we're scaling that with technology, which frees up my time elsewhere."

Rather than be derailed by volatility right at the beginning of his career, Dr. Scott instead doubled down on his teaching, marketing, and leadership skill sets, which gave him exponentially more opportunities. In a short time, Dr. Scott was able to own his freedom—not because of his technical training but because of his additional skill sets that had nothing to do with his technical skills learned from his years of formal education.

Dr. Scott was able to own his freedom— not because of his technical training, but because of his additional skill sets.

"At first, I was pushed into it more outside of my comfort zone because of my injury. Had I been a good dentist and made good enough money and had a schedule that didn't kill me, I might've never left the rat race. When I was pushed, I didn't fall down. I started running forward, relying on my other skills. And every time I'd run forward, I'd stumble. For whatever reason, I decided to actually make a good thing out of every stumble. Learn from it, teach it, act on it to do better—don't hit a wall and overanalyze it."

These circumstances literally changed his life. Even though he experienced some fear, and anxiety when he started down this path, in the long run, it turned out to be a blessing.

Now, Scott truly is owning his freedom: "Sometimes I build new companies. Sometimes I go help my kids' elementary school, sometimes I get in better shape. Sometimes I travel with my wife, sometimes I do nothing." He's doing what he wants to when he wants to, with whom he wants—and loving it.

No matter what type of entrepreneur, business owner, or practice owner we are, *most of us get stuck in the skills that are unique to our business.* Our formal or technical training in our career profession is in large part based on specialized skills. Whether you're a marketer, physical therapist, or writer, you spend most of your time working to develop and improve your technical craft.

We don't spend much time getting outside-the-box skills. I'm guilty of that myself sometimes. In my case, dentistry is very, very specialized. To work as a dentist, I must have specialized training, practice in a dental office, and serve customers directly in front of me. On the surface, there's not much room for variation. So the more I specialize, the better I can serve my customers, right?

While you're trading your time for more dollars, you're not gaining any more freedom. The problem with an overdependence on specialization is that it leaves us vulnerable. To depend solely on specialization is akin to putting all your eggs in one basket. If that basket were to fall from your hands, you'd have a mess.

In a volatile economy, were the rapidly changing landscape to disrupt your specialized business, you'd likewise be vulnerable—extremely fragile.

Thankfully, we can develop other, generalized skills beyond those of our specialization. This isn't easy. That's why, when I talk about the principles of freedom with business owners and entrepreneurs, one of my favorite topics is this fifth principle: *transferable skill sets.*

Transferable skill sets help you own and sustain your freedom. When Scott lost his ability to practice dentistry, he shifted his focus to teaching, marketing, and leadership, bringing in customers and other practitioners to deliver his services. He now has transferable skills he could use anywhere.

Everywhere, people are more mobile. No longer do we see the thirty-year career at one company as standard. Fewer professionals are climbing one corporate ladder. This increased mobility includes skills. In your career, income, and life, the more mobile you are, the better you're able to sustain wealth in a disruptive environment. If you have skills that you can transfer from one opportunity to another, then you can sustain your freedom in a volatile world.

In my case, I am a product of the product. I began my early adult life in pursuit of advanced degrees that eventually produced my dental license and the right and ability to practice dentistry. This was the goal and I had at last achieved it.

Thankfully, my own curiosity and desire to learn outside of my "chosen profession" provided me with multiple options and skill sets that allowed me to pivot when I needed that ability most (when Jenna was sick, when I failed in my first attempt at my practice sale, and when I began the organic formation of Freedom Founders in 2010).

My early ventures in real estate led me to many new skill sets for which I had zero academic or formal training. Marketing, sales, negotiation, finance, legal contracts, deal orchestration, and problem solving—exactly what our public school system does *not* teach, yet these are skills that are adaptable to so many different constructs, situations, or opportunities.

Don't get me wrong. I am proud and appreciative of the training I received as a dentist and the blessing to help so many people with solutions to their oral problems. This was very satisfying…to a degree. But I could always feel the beat of a different drummer inside, and real estate, the entrepreneurial life, and the vision of those in this tribe was the rhythm I'd been searching for.

I became entranced with "the art of the deal." Negotiating the solutions to solve other people's problems while allowing me to build an asset base that would in a relatively short time set me free was a gamechanger. I love solving problems that create asset-based income (the real estate investments), which eventually became the financial foundation of my Plan B.

As a final note on the subject of the game-changing skills we must learn, the best gift you could give to your children or grandchildren will not be money and will not be a paid-for academic education. I'm not opposed to some level of either one, but learning real life skill sets that are transferable to an endless number of businesses or opportunities is *THE WAY* to navigate the volatile times we have ahead.

Don't miss this point! Degrees and licenses become irrelevant about the time the graduate crosses the stage. All of the principles that Dan and I have laid out in this book are for the creation and maintenance of personal freedom and autonomy in a world that is focused on taking that away from you! Please don't miss the message!

What Stage Are You in Your Entrepreneurial Evolution?

As Dan describes in "Chapter 3: The Evolution of a Free Person," business owners and entrepreneurs go through several stages throughout their career span. Here I'll describe how such "evolution" relates to our entrepreneurial skills.

We start hunched over on all fours, nose to the grindstone, applying ourselves to our technical training and specialized skills. We're a *worker* on the front line. We may work for somebody else until we get to a point where we start a company or business of our own.

When that happens, we take a step forward, rise a bit upright. We start seeing things a little bit differently. Even so, we're still a *business operator*, which means while we own the business, we're still doing a lot of the business's actual productivity.

Business owner is the next big step up when we reach the point where we have others doing more of the actual labor, performing the *technical work or services*. You may be doing some, but at a level where you're working more *on* the business and less *in* the business.

At that point, the business owner might start looking at the business's marketing, which is terra incognita for many technical specialists. Fewer business owners reach this stage because most have the attitude: "I do good work and provide great services, so people will just pound my door down for work." Well, that's not necessarily the case.

You've got to market your excellent services or products. In the process of elevating to a *marketer*, you'll gain a big transferable skill set—this is typically the first new set of skills a specialist has gained outside their profession in a long time.

The skillset you gain could be something niche: social media marketing, writing good copy, or direct mail, for example. Whatever it is, it's a step in the right direction—a new skill you can use in capacities beyond those of your specialization.

The second to last stage is a *skilled entrepreneur* who is adding skill sets on top of skill sets. On top of marketing, they're investing in their leadership, HR, and more, becoming a business leader able to orchestrate the culture of the company—which allows them to do little of the business's work. They're instead responsible for putting the right people, the right culture, and the right systems and processes in place.

For example, a dental practice owner in an entrepreneur capacity gets really good at the systems and processes of running a really great experience for the patients, they've got a good system for treatment evaluations, a great process for providing the treatment, and financial options. They've dialed all these processes to the point where they're not the ones who are doing it, but they have the processes. This has given them a slew of transferable skill sets.

Now what? Could they transfer those same processes to something else?

Perhaps they decide to open a kiosk in the mall that does just whitening. No dental services, only whitening specialized treatment. Well, that's a transferable skillset for which the entrepreneur knows how to hire, how to find the right location, how to market, how to put in place the right systems and processes, and more.

Such adaptability and flexibility in your skills provide you multiple streams of income. You become that business entrepreneur who sees opportunity from a higher-level playing field.

Finally, the last piece of this evolution is becoming an *investor*. As an investor, not actively involved in a particular investment, be it a business or real estate, you are putting your capital in with somebody else who you've decided has a good model and asset. (Of course, you can be both an entrepreneur and an investor at the same time.)

Not everybody has to climb all the way to the final stage of entrepreneur-investor. Some people might be very happy staying at the business operator or business owner level because they really love that it allows them to own their freedom—as long as they don't have all their eggs in one basket.

You're somewhere on that journey. Most are probably at the point where they're an owner involved in some marketing but aren't certain of the best way forward. Once you know where you are, you can see how to go forward.

Why the Worst Number Is "One"

What's the worst number in business? One. One primary customer to rely on. One referral partner sending business your way. One service to sell. One specialty at risk of the next disruption. One producer trading hours for dollars.

You don't want to limit yourself to *one* of anything. It's dangerous. It leaves you in a fragile, more vulnerable position in life and in your personal freedom. If you have one source of clients, that's all your eggs in one basket. What happens if that go-to referral source dries up? How could multiple streams of revenue be better?

During the Covid-19 shutdown, our Freedom Founders members were thankful they had outside assets that produced income, even though their primary income was shut down 6-8 weeks. Those who relied on "one" struggled.

What Are Your Transferable Strengths?

Transferable skill sets are those you can develop in your primary business and later apply to secondary income streams—in particular, those that generate passive income so you don't have to be trading time for dollars.

The whole point of applying your transferable skill sets is so they can free you up to *not* trade your time for dollars. Developing a second income stream (or even multiple) with these general skill sets allows you to spend less time on active income while providing more passive cash flow.

The key here is that this is not a typical way of thinking. Most people think they must put all their focus on formal education, developing formal technical skills.

Technical experts with specialized skills could devote time to developing such transferable skill sets as:

- ▶ Writing
- ▶ Communication
- ▶ Critical thinking
- ▶ Creativity
- ▶ Marketing
- ▶ Sales
- ▶ Negotiation
- ▶ Problem-solving
- ▶ Management
- ▶ Leadership

We're *not* taught to think outside the box. We're taught that specialization is the key to freedom. We're comfortable with our specialized skill set, and the rest is territory for other people, not us. So we box ourselves in by leaving these other skills undeveloped, even though generalized skills can increase our effectiveness in many others areas of our business.

Thankfully, developing transferable skills is relatively straightforward. You're not taught these skills in your industry, so don't go looking for them there. When I go to a dental education conference or seminar, they're not typically teaching me other skill sets. They're teaching me what they think we need to know to be the best technical operators.

I have to go outside of my industry to develop these skills. I find other venues, groups, reading materials that help give me the skill set.

I have to go outside of my industry to develop these skills.

The key is, I want to do it. I've got to be a seeker. I've got to have an innate curiosity within me that says, "I'm using my technical skills to leapfrog to another place in my career path, which allows for additional streams of income, which gets me closer to freedom."

Strengths Assessment

▶ What are your strengths? What non-technical work do you enjoy?

▶ What are the transferable skill sets related to your strengths and what you enjoy?

▶ How could you further develop these skills?

▶ Which skill(s) could you apply to a new income stream?

▶ How could these transferable skill sets provide more opportunities for freedom?

Everyone's skill set is different. There's no reason you should try to make your strengths the same as anybody else. In fact, if you have a strength not shared by many others, this could be a competitive advantage.

Be honest with yourself. Know where you spend time in your daily activities. If you love doing something, could it be a transferable skill? For example: writing or speaking in front of a group; teaching or mentoring; could you apply these to another income stream? If so, that's one of your strengths. Invest in it.

The Independence to *Own* Your Freedom

"Invest in Transferable Skill Sets" is one of five principles in this book because it significantly contributes to providing sustainable wealth in a volatile world. It supports the "sustainability" aspect of your wealth.

Dependence on one skill is anti-freedom. You are vulnerable if you are dependent on any one thing – one primary source of income, one business, one job, one career – or at the mercy of any outside force, such as government regulation.

The government is very quick and doesn't hold back when those in charge decide they want to regulate an industry in the name of control. In the same vein, you may rely on a group or a trade association to do the heavy lifting to "protect" your industry. Well, none of those outside forces really care as much about your freedom as much as you do. Everybody has their own agenda, and it rarely is one that provides *you* more freedom and independence.

There are benefits to government, groups, and associations. But we must be careful not to become dependent on those outside forces or agencies. If we do, then we are leaving our freedoms susceptible.

It's more important today, probably more than ever before, that we as individuals or family members develop as much independence as we can. Why? Because of society's current push towards *dependency*.

In the US and around the globe, governments have more power than ever. The government sustains power by having more and more people dependent on it. When more of us rely solely on government, we leave ourselves exposed.

We must avoid getting sucked into hoping that the government will provide our Social Security checks (even though it's an upside-down Ponzi scheme) or that Medicare will cover our every need (even though it doesn't).

If you don't have your own wealth platform built up with multiple streams of income and ability, with enough wealth to provide for you to live, then you are going to become dependent.

Once you're dependent, your freedom is taken away. You might have some false sense of security, but you don't have the freedom to do what you want when you want—which is how we define our freedom in this book.

Plus, what you're dependent *on* can disappear or change overnight.

> ## Once you're dependent, your freedom is taken away.

Marketing as a Transferable Skill

How many businesses out there in the world today have a good product or service but do not know how to show their potential prospects or potential customers what it is they do? The offering fails because they don't market it. It happens every day.

Dan Kennedy always says that the elevation from business operator to business marketer is a big step. When people do it, they start looking at their business completely differently. Marketing really is the essence of being a business owner.

Thankfully, marketing is a learned skill.

One of the things that we love to do in Freedom Founders is our program called The Apprentice Program. It's built off of the book I wrote, *The Apprentice Model*, where I recommend this very concept of transferable skill sets. The premise: *Don't get so sucked into a career path early in life that you don't have a chance to explore a little bit and see what your strengths are.*

One young man we had as an apprentice had a maturity beyond his years. He was marketing savvy and an excellent communicator. I wondered: *Did he start out this way?*

Turns out, he had a similar background to mine. In college, even though he was an introvert, he waited tables for the money. "I learned so much about how to communicate with different kinds of people, an experience I wouldn't have gotten anywhere else. Waiting tables was like a laboratory for me to up my game with communication."

The young man loved his newfound ability to communicate so much that he graduated with a degree in marketing. Today, as a young professional, he uses his marketing and communication skills every day. These skills will serve him no matter what specialized industries he works within.

Why are transferable skill sets like marketing so important for smaller business owners? Marketing drives sales through engagement and differentiation. Without customers and sales, the best technician will not survive. And you can't sell your business at top value while being just a commodity.

Your Business Is More than a Commodity

It's a shifting world. Whether you shift to take advantage of a new opportunity or to survive disruption, at some point, every small business owner needs to shift their business to survive. Such a shift requires much more than the technical skills we are taught.

Technical and specialized skill sets are built into the heart of your business. It's what your customers pay for directly. Transferable skills, on the other hand, aren't built-in from the beginning. They must be acquired with intention. This is a difficult concept to embrace when we've been taught that a focus on specialized skills is the path to freedom.

The more you stay in the same place, doing what everyone else is doing, the more you commoditize your business. And when you're a commodity, you're no different from anybody else. At that level, you're just competing on price, which is the worst place to be. Only a Goliath with leverage, like Wal-Mart, survives when competing on price. Smaller businesses can't do that.

The more you stay in the same place, doing what everyone else is doing, the more you commoditize your business.

Today, many industries are being commoditized. Especially in the healthcare space, where insurance has taken over—dentistry, veterinary medicine, chiropractic, optical, optometry, pharmacy, physical therapy—every offering has become the "same" in the eyes of most consumers, who shop on "who takes my insurance" or "who's got the cheapest service."

So, if you're a provider trying to be all things to all people yet you're not the cheapest, you'll lose business. Instead, look at ways to connect or engage with a certain niche of your clientele. Your efforts should create an experience and long-term relationships with the target customer or client that you wish to serve.

Communication, marketing skills, building out systems and processes, a celebrated culture—these skill sets allow you to be more adaptable and flexible with your own business model. You can stay above the fray, not be pummeled by price, and dodge the other outside forces continually pushing commoditization.

"Do I Really Need *More* Skills?"

You may have some hesitation: do I really need multiple, different skill sets? I have only so many hours in the day.

The short answer is yes—as long as these additional transferable skill sets contribute to you owning your freedom.

Think of investing in your transferable skills as like investing in assets—it's your human capital. Your transferable skills are volatility-proof. They will stay with you no matter how your business fluctuates. Other assets you can lose. But these are skill sets that never can be taken away from you once you have them.

Even more, the more you invest in transferable skill sets, the bigger the eventual payoff.

In late 2020, I was on a call with one of our smaller groups, a mix of practice or business owners: doctors, dentists, financial planners. The variety of experiences is fun because it gives us a wider perspective than that of any one industry.

Despite the variety, everyone on the call agreed with one big point: for their business to survive the Covid-19 crisis, they'd had to rely on a great deal of skills they hadn't learned in their technical training. And yet, because they'd developed or were willing to develop these transferable skill sets, they were able to face the worst.

One example: one of our newer members and his wife are both orthopedic surgeons. They have elevated themselves both out of actually seeing patients. He has three offices in Chicago. He shared how he has not physically been in any of his offices in the previous three weeks.

Now, how can he, a business owner, do everything remotely?

Running three offices remotely wasn't part of his surgical training. But even though he is a very talented surgeon, he made a decision a while back that he didn't want to be *dependent* on surgery.

So he developed skill sets in marketing, culture, systems, processes, and leadership.

For instance, the couple has focused marketing on non-surgical intervention—all the therapies you can do before you go and get a hip or joint replacement. This focus has generated a huge amount of new business. With his transferable skill sets, he turned one income source into multiple income streams.

By thinking of the business as more than just a medium for their technical skills, the couple was able to see a big opportunity. Now, they use their technical training in a different capacity. Instead of performing the work, their understanding of the technical side allows them to know quality. They know what they want in services, employees, and resources—who can perform and what it takes to perform. They're the best evaluator of their own business because of their baseline technical understanding.

That said, even though they have multiple offices, they still have a concern—much of their revenue is regulated to a great degree by government healthcare like Medicare. They sensed a vulnerability. That's why they joined Freedom Founders. Now they're also investing in real estate because they want to continue to diversify beyond their actual business venture.

Transferable Skill Sets to Sustain Your Freedom

We learned in previous chapters how investing in real estate is a way to diversify your assets. By the same token, investing in your transferable skill sets is a way to diversify your productive activities. Such investing and diversification allow you to become more independent and anti-fragile— putting you well on the path to owning your freedom.

We can't become complacent, even in good times. We can't expect everything's going to remain good because things always change. The economy could implode. Or Amazon could disrupt your market forever. The government could create a new regulation you didn't see coming. Or, like Dr. Scott Leune, you could have an accident and lose your ability to perform your specialized work.

Once you've developed a transferable skill set, you can apply it to other ventures, whether in good times or bad. These skills give you peace of mind. So invest in them. Because, no matter what happens, you'll have more freedom with these skills than without.

CHAPTER 11

THE POWER OF "BEFORE YOU ARE READY"

BY DAN S. KENNEDY

hen two gunfighters met in the center of Main Street at high noon, one didn't courteously say to the other, "Draw your gun when you're ready." There, facing off, life or death, there could be *no* waiting until you felt ready.

Most modern threats aren't any more courteous, nor are most opportunities. One of the richest men I got to spend an interesting evening with in Las Vegas, by happy accident, said, at one point, "There are countless sensible, defensible reasons for waiting, and that means avoiding, and then there is acting. They are basically two different things. Habitually lived by two different people."

The Risks of "Not"

By *not* doing things, people try to eliminate risks. If you never go sky-diving, you eliminate the risk of dying from a parachute malfunction, and for most people, giving up parachute jumping for Lent is not that big of a sacrifice. However, President Bush famously almost choked to death eating a pretzel. You could decide, made aware of that risk, not to eat pretzels. But to entirely eliminate the risk of choking to death you have to give up eating altogether, and that obviously bears greater and more certain risk than does eating.

You could eliminate the risk of injury or death in a car accident by never going anywhere in an automobile, but that decision would bear many risks and certain costs, possibly including prohibition of needed medical care. Instead, you make *risk mitigation decisions* about going places in automobiles. And you may make more stringent or less stringent ones than I do. We could, as a society, get to zero auto accident fatalities, by setting all speed limits at 5 MPH and requiring everyone to drive a Hummer. We don't do this because the risks to our economy, our mobility, our food supply, our health, etc., are too great. So we accept that we are going to kill a certain number of people every year with cars. This *was* debated (!) when we switched from horses 'n buggies. But we have long ago agreed to accept that our use of automobiles means a certain number of deaths every year.

Mike Rowe, former host of the reality TV show DIRTY JOBS, has an interesting take on all this, born of our fight with the Covid-19 pandemic response, he has labeled "SAFETY <u>THIRD</u>" – in place of the common "Safety First." His thoughts are worth hearing. You can, at https://mikerowe.com

In business, there is risk in delegation; risks of disappointment, unintentional harm, deliberate betrayal, and more; legal, financial, reputational, and more. Yet it is nearly impossible to function without engaging in some delegation, so we each make risk mitigation decisions about who we delegate what to, how we delegate and supervise and verify. I have written about delegation elsewhere in this book, but it is a good analogy to investing and even to managing some investing risks; you can*not* advance very far without delegation or without managed investment risk.

YOU CANNOT ADVANCE VERY FAR WITHOUT DELEGATION OR WITHOUT MANAGED INVESTMENT RISK.

The chief risk of NOT investing and of NOT having your money deployed in investments is inflation. In best times, it slowly, somewhat sneakily erodes the spending power of your dollar saved in a shoebox underneath your bed. In worse times, it quickly erases big hunks of that value. At only 4 percent yearly inflation applied to saved dollars held with zero risk, in just 12-1/2 years you've lost 50 percent of those dollars' actual worth to you. In reality, inflation is a *certain* risk. Investment loss is *not* a certain risk, and it is a risk YOU can act to manage and mitigate. Wealth, personal economic autonomy, and ongoing income from saved money rather than active labor all *require* risks, to be understood and managed (not avoided).

You Will Fall Off A Financial Horse, Probably More Than Once, But It Is Extremely Rare For It To Be "Fatal," If You Have Taken Reasonable Precautions

I was backstage a number of times as a speaker with Christopher Reeve, the actor known for playing Superman in the movies, paralyzed in a horse-riding accident. He was confined to a high-tech wheelchair and breathing apparatus, so traveling to one of these events to speak was not only arduous but risky. Once I overheard a reporter ask him if, knowing what he knows now, he would have avoided being on horseback. He answered, "No. I would have made more of a point of *staying on* horseback." It was a pre-scripted answer to an often-asked question, meant to lighten the moment. But it also spoke to the risks inherent in living life to its fullest in the context of personal interests and ambitions or with investing to achieve replacement of active, earned income with passive income or with just deciding to get in your car and go – without smart preparation and precautions. It is a dangerous world out there!

The biggest risk to your financial freedom is doing nothing. The second biggest risk is doing little and doing it late. The best time to start playing catch-up if you must, or to moving ahead toward financial freedom, is now. That may seem to be acting BEFORE you are ready. You may think *"it would be better to wait until <fill in the blank> before making any changes."* The trouble with that is there is *always* a fill-in-the-blank answer, *always* a reason to wait, to procrastinate, to postpone. There is an old, rather morbid joke about this, about the elderly couple standing before the judge in Divorce Court. The judge says: "Harry, you are 86. Helen, you are 82. You've been married for 61 years. Why on God's green earth are you in my court now?" And Harry says, "We've been waiting for the kids to die."

I *know* you don't laugh at that. You cringe. I've been telling it for many years despite knowing it's not going to get robust laughter. I know it makes people uncomfortable.

Wealth and financial freedom are almost always attracted and built by doing things *before* you are ready AND by doing things that feel "uncomfortable." That can include something as innocuous as reading Investor's Business Daily every day or at least every weekend edition before you are ready to actually start developing an investment portfolio. Or reading real estate-related periodicals before you are ready to invest in properties. Having and feeding such interests, at the very least, leads you to the "doing" sooner than later, leads to action faster. But it can also include much more significant moves made before you are ready. Elsewhere in this book, you got my Arnold Schwarzenegger story and Dr. Phelps story, both of actually starting to make real estate investments well before they would be considered ready by others – but, to their credit, because they decided waiting was NOT a winning strategy.

With this book, by the way, if you only read it but then do nothing about it or because of it, now, not later "when you are ready", we have all failed; Dr. Phelps, me, and you.

THE 90 DAY EXPERIMENT THAT COULD CHANGE YOUR RELATIONSHIP WITH MONEY FOREVER

There is a specific before-you-are-ready "system of financial behavior" that I'm going to recommend to you here, presented in abbreviated form, with the hope that you will trust me enough to try a 90-Day Experiment with it. That's all it will take for it to prove itself to you, no matter how strange or counterintuitive it may seem at the start. The strategy involves making pre-set by percentage payments to a Wealth Account and a Giving Account, off the top of any and all dollars that come to you, no matter their source, and regardless of your present financial circumstances. Please re-read that instruction to be certain you understand its "absolutes." It allows no exceptions.

To execute this strategy, you establish two new bank accounts, one designated as your Wealth Account, the other as your Giving Account. You determine the percentage to be skimmed off the top of *all* monies coming to you for each account's deposits. You may, for example, make them both 1 percent or both 5 percent, or only 1 percent to Giving and 9 percent to Wealth, or any other mix. The mandate is to lock in the percentage skimmed off the top and deposited to each of these accounts. Depending on how frequently money comes to you, you will need to do daily or weekly or, at longest, bi-weekly deposits to both accounts. In the early going, to those with professional practices or retail businesses, I recommend daily. From the Wealth Account, there can be no withdrawals during The 90-Day Experiment, and continuing beyond that only transfers to investments made for gains or yield. From the Giving Account, you can make any legitimate charitable payments you prefer, to your church, non-profit organizations, or an individual or individuals in need. It's important not to cheat with any of this – you cheat yourself!

The Wealth Account seems logical, of course, but the Giving Account does not. If you have $100 come in and you move it to a Wealth Account, you still have it, but if you give it away, you do *not* have it, so how the dickens can that help your wealth? One of the strangest things you will discover with this strategy is that both of the accounts are actually Wealth Accounts! This strategy has you doing – and not waiting until you are ready – the two things that wealthy people do with the money that comes to them: assigning percentages to investment and to charity or philanthropy. **By doing these two things, you condition your conscious and subconscious minds to the idea that you are a wealthy person, your internal "harmful stuff" about money is replaced by the consciousness of a wealthy person, and you magnetically attract money by engaging in the behaviors it approves of.** It is perfectly okay to begin your 90 Day Experiment with this as a skeptic. What you believe about it won't stop it from working any more than disbelieving in gravity will make you weightless.

Incidentally, when this was first explained to me by a successful teacher named Foster Hibbard[4] almost exactly as I have explained it here, I thought it was "crazy talk" and I was not flush with extra cash, needed every incoming dollar for current expenses, and could not afford skimming any percentage off the top, but I somewhat grudgingly and doubtfully did it anyway – before I was ready or able. The results, with no other variables to explain them, were astonishing. This became a permanent regimen for me, and one that I have shared with many thousands of other people, and, from many, have gotten their reports of astonishing results.

If you would like more on this, from a Christian perspective, I recommend the book *THE GENEROSITY SECRET* by Nelson Searcy. Nelson is a friend of mine, the founding and lead pastor of

---

4 Foster Hibbard was a close associate of Napoleon Hill's for some years, a stock broker, and then a very popular lecturer and author in the professions of chiropractic and dentistry. I built a national seminar business featuring Foster in the 1980s, presenting evening "money seminars" to doctors in every state but Hawaii and Alaska multiple times.

The Journey Church with locations in New York and Florida. He is also the President of ChurchLeaderInsights.com and The Renegade Pastors Network, an international coaching and mastermind program.

This is part and parcel of BEING rich BEFORE you are or are ready to be rich. This should NOT be confused with what is often, unfortunately, taught as "fake it 'til you make it." That is aimed at the outside world. It has you "faking it" to others, typically by going into debt for "appearances," and it is costly and dangerous. If used at all, by the seeming necessity of a particular business, it should be used sparingly, with the wary understanding that you are playing with financial fire. What I have prescribed is aimed at you, not at others' perceptions or opinions. Its purpose is to fundamentally alter and strengthen your relationship with money, not to impress anyone else. It is private, not public. It has you paying you first, not racking up debt and paying credit card companies. This is not about play-acting wealthy; it is about being wealthy. Andrew Carnegie, one of America's first-ever billionaires from scratch, said that wealth is *made* in the minds and behaviors of a man, then *collected* in the physical world.

Ultimately, the more ways you (carefully, not recklessly) move toward wealth and act to attract wealth before you are ready, the faster you will actually be wealthy in real terms.

It's important to remember that time is the most perishable asset you have, but it is the asset that enables or hampers, speeds or slows the achievement of every goal and the acquisition of every other asset. An equal amount is given to each person each day. Different life experiences and financial situations come from its good use, poor use, or non-use. You can't wait until you are ready to proceed with "x", and bank time to accumulate, to be taken off the shelf and used at your convenience when you finally feel ready. The shelf will be empty.

Further, there are unseen urgencies inherent in just about every set of circumstances, including finances.

One of my favorite billionaires, W. Clement Stone, used the term "*inspiration to action.*" Stone said that you could predict a man's success, stagnation, or failure, and you could judge a man's likelihood of achieving stated goals by how quickly he acted whenever provided relevant inspiration. I often tell Lee Iacocca's story of his returning the convertible to American roads while CEO of Chrysler, during that company's arduous climb out of a deep financial hole. I visited with Iacocca on several occasions while working on one project. He said he was walking the factory floor one day when a working man called out to him, pointed at the "K-car" sedans they were making then, and said, "This isn't a great car but it would make a great convertible." Iacocca said, "Think so? Get a blowtorch and cut the roof off of one of them, we'll take a drive over by the college campus, and see if girls look at it at stoplights, park, and see if guys come up and ask us about it. If they do, we'll make 'em." Stone would give Iacocca high, high marks for inspiration-to-action.

Conversely, inspiration *without* action is almost entirely wasted. Sparks briefly fly, but no lasting fires are made. Lives are not changed by inspiration; they are only changed by inspiration to action.

If you have been inspired by this book, if you are intrigued or motivated or hopeful or optimistic about grabbing your financial bull by its horns, the time to do something about it is now. Before the inspiration flickers and fades and dies. Amongst the *immediate* actions you might take—amongst the actions you *can take immediately*— would be contacting Dr. Phelps's Freedom Founders group and investigating its potential appropriateness for you.

It Might Be "Early," But That's A Whole Lot Better Than "Too Late"

You may only have *a desire* for financial freedom and for financial strengthening in your life – *not a need*. From unpleasant personal experience, I can tell you that the possibility of sudden, surprise need lurks, and if it has not been taken care of in advance it can prove devilishly difficult to manage after its fact. In 2019, suddenly, with no significant warning (other than having a chronic but apparently stable and non-threatening health condition), I was struck down just about overnight, facing a convergence of medical crises, in the hospital, in the ICU, then out, saved but facing such a daunting mountain that I entered hospice fully intending to die in a matter of weeks. After weeks and recovery of some functions, I exited hospice. My subsequent rehab was roughly eight months long and arduous.

From a financial standpoint, I went from merrily sailing along earning a 7-figure income, requiring only one staff person, and with a great deal of business on the books for 6 to 18 months into the future, deposits banked, to – pardon the expression – a dead stop. Zero income. Refunds of deposits and fees for which services could not be completed topping $400,000. Despite excellent health insurance, a still dizzying blizzard of new expenses, including home health care services, accrued. Fortunately, I had long ago passed the point of working for active, earned income out of need. Instead, I had *zero* debt, wealth – much of it secure – and a "system" for managing The Business of My Money that my wife could operate. I had plenty of problems, but money wasn't one of them. Had it been, I cannot imagine how we would have gotten through it all. To borrow from,

I think, Totie Fields: "I've been broke and I've been rich, and rich is better"—even in these other misery-inducing circumstances.

I am, now, as recovered as I will be, most problems resolved or reduced to the level of annoyances to be managed, the worst permanent impairment with vision. Mini-strokes in my eyes made one permanently blind, the other impaired.

You may never have anything comparable – medically – occur in your life, and I sincerely hope you don't. If it has a silver lining, it has eluded me. However, you may have noticed the recent Covid-19 pandemic and its spurring of draconian lockdowns and severe disruption to many businesses, including professional practices, suddenly, without warning, changing many from thriving to barely surviving or worse.

The harsh reality is any one of us or all of us are never far removed and certainly never entirely safe from some yanking of what felt like solid ground out from under us.

We routinely take "solid ground" for granted, and maybe we need to in order to live without constant fear and worry, and to go about our daily lives, but this does not negate the fact of a long list of sudden horrors that may arrive in one's life at any moment. Once we had Mickey Dolenz, one of The Monkees, as a guest celebrity at one of our members' conferences the day after the entire town he lived in, Paradise, California was engulfed by a wildfire and burned to the ground. He told me that firefighters arrived at his door and told him he had five minutes to gather things he wanted to take, then he *was* leaving with them. I expressed my gratitude that he was with us and frank surprise that he hadn't canceled, and he shrugged and said, "Why cancel on you? I really didn't have anywhere else to be." This, as hard as it can be to imagine, can, in fact, be the situation you or I confront: having nowhere else to be but in sudden crisis or its aftermath, having to re-construct the life we live. Better not to have to re-construct your finances from ashes, too.

With this in mind, postponing constructive action on making the strongest financial fortress possible, even for a day, is ill-advised. Even one day's better start may put you ahead of some future unpleasant surprise rather than leaving you nakedly unprepared for it.

CHAPTER 12

OWN YOUR FREEDOM, IN GOOD TIMES AND BAD

BY DR. DAVID PHELPS

"You may not control all the events that happen to you, but you can decide not to be reduced by them."

Maya Angelou, Poet

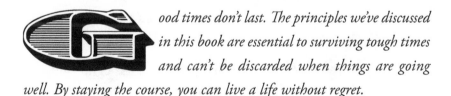 ood times don't last. *The principles we've discussed in this book are essential to surviving tough times and can't be discarded when things are going well. By staying the course, you can live a life without regret.*

FREEDOM QUESTIONS:

....

In tough times, do you work toward more security or more freedom? And, when times are good, is bigger always better? How are you preparing for tough times today? What do you really want—to chase opportunity or to start building your legacy now?

Jeremy Tate, a young marketer and business owner, is part of our mastermind group, "Collective Genius," which focuses on real estate. In the fall of 2020, he wrote on the group's webpage forum, looking for advice:

"Hey genius family. I've struggled for the last six or seven days deciding whether to open up about this or not. And now it's hurting so bad that I don't have a choice. I literally feel like I have a thousand-pound weight on my shoulders right now. It's causing all kinds of stress, bad emotions, and I'm finding it impossible to get off my mind. We have more clients than we ever had. We're making more money than we ever had. We have a bigger team than we ever had. Our systems and processes in our teams are performing better than ever. But we're drowning and drowning quickly. Here's the vulnerable part: I have two maxed out credit cards that I could only make the minimum payment for this month. We're going to owe thirty thousand in taxes for this year that I don't have saved up. I barely made payroll for my team last week and have no clue how I'm going to do it for

the coming week. Expenses are higher than ever. This is also now affecting my personal finances. I have a credit card maxed out and close to nothing in my account. It's kept me up at night. I might have an emotional breakdown today."

Jeremy Tate is a vibrant young man who, from the outside, has all the chops. He has a passion for what he does, and he's very good at it. On the surface, it might've looked like things were going well, but he grew too fast. He goes on:

"This time last year, we had a fourth of the clients, and we were making a fourth of the money. But we were profiting more than we are now. So this issue is brand new. It's something we've never had a problem with."

Jeremy Tate benefited from a good economy. In 2019, the favorable climate created good times, making it seem like the success would never end. More clients wanting services. Easier cash flow. Spending without much second thought. Business tends to grow in these times.

Jeremy did a great job riding this wave. He built a business, earned a sparkling reputation, and took care of his people.

But still he grew too fast.

Growth sucks cash. As you grow, you eventually get to the point where your overhead is so high that the only thing that can keep you afloat is more and more new cash. If the economy dips and cash stalls, the overhead can be crushing.

That's what happened in 2020.

Jeremy found he was trying to serve too many clients in too many ways. Figuring that out and paring back those services would help reduce the overhead. But in the midst of crushing stress and overstretched responsibilities it can be difficult to see the best way forward.

Thankfully, Jeremy was willing to be vulnerable at a time when most people are prideful. Few of us would ever want to show our cards like he did in front of a group—because there's an expectation that if you're part of such a group, then you've got to be good. You've got to always maintain the *appearance* of success, right?

Wrong. Success is being willing to accept setbacks as part and parcel of the entrepreneurial journey while staying ready to pivot (changing strategies or tactics) after considering the options. Success is learning from feedback and making a course correction when you need to.

During bad times, the mistake many make is to yield to anxiety, panic, and fear. They make decisions that buy some temporary security at the expense of profit and their future freedom. One needs to be very careful of not making decisions that will negatively affect their future—consumer debt being one example. Even during bad times there remain good options, so you don't have to accept less in return for the promise of stability.

In Jeremy's case, I was proud of our membership group. Very quickly, many jumped in and said, "Whoa, time out. No judgment here. We've all been there. Glad you're opening up here, in a place where you can get clarity, feedback, and belonging, so you don't feel all alone in trying to deal with these challenges."

Isn't that marvelous? A group of hyper-successful business owners, all of whom have experienced crushing setbacks, taking the time to help one another.

It's not weakness to ask for help—in fact, it's part of what makes you stronger in the long run. Until we are willing to be vulnerable, it's

226   OwnYourFreedomBook.com

difficult to change. Being prideful is just one example of being your own worst enemy. Get out of your own way. Allow others to help.

We all need to hear this advice at some point, especially when the good times turn bad and we're realizing we made a slew of decisions that don't look so good in hindsight.

In this chapter, we'll learn the same thing Jeremy did: we must sustain the same approach in good times and bad. Resist the temptation to ditch the five principles just because you "think" you can afford to. Hold true to yourself. You'll thank yourself when the tough times come around again.

We must sustain the same approach in good times and bad.

The Bad Times: We All Make Mistakes

Fifteen years ago, I was motivated to sell my dental practice because of my daughter's health situation. I was so motivated that I didn't follow the prudent rules of selling. Big mistake.

What happened was that I elected to provide financing (carry the note)on the sale of the practice to the young buyer. Then the whole deal fell apart. I had to take back the practice through litigation. It was messy and emotional. I took a lot of money out of savings in other assets to float the boat.

At a low point, I wondered: *What went wrong? Where did I mess up? How could this happen to me?*

I spoke to my circle of trusted friends. I like to use the word *friend* because these aren't just people I do business with—they're those who I know and trust. This group of four or five I can go to and say, "Hey, I'm in a tough spot here, and I'm not sure exactly what I need to do to fix this. Do I walk away from the practice? Do I pour more money into it? Do I keep fighting this? I'm a little bit lost in the weeds here, and I just need some perspective from third parties to figure it out."

What did I learn about my mistake? It's never as bad as we think. Whatever the situation is at the outset, whatever it is that we face, it seems scary at first because it's new to us. It blindsides you, then, all of a sudden, bam! You feel like you've been thrown into the hole.

But it's never as bad as we think. So lesson number one: *Don't go into panic mode.*

That means you don't make quick or rash decisions based on the current circumstances. Instead, pause and look around. Who's in your network? Who's your board of advisors. Who have you built relationship capital with and who could give you some perspective? They'll help you see what to prioritize as you dig out.

In tough times, the natural reaction for most people is to start doubling down on security, drifting further and further away from freedom. That's our knee-jerk response.

> # In tough times, the natural reaction for most people is to start doubling down on security, drifting further and further away from freedom.

If it's not our pride, it's often the "sunk cost" fallacy—we're into something so deep we don't see the benefits of just cutting our losses.

With my practice, it was my baby. I'd owned and operated it for twenty years. I had a lot of emotional and financial capital invested in it. Could I just walk away and call it a day after raising the baby for two decades? That's really hard to do.

Jeremy was in a similar boat. He likewise had invested significant emotional and financial capital. He felt, to some degree, responsible for his employees. He also had cherished clients to whom he was trying to deliver.

Should he have tried to just work harder? Lesson number two: *when you face these situations, just working harder in the same model is not a plan.*

That's why you need perspective. You need someone else to give you some guidance or permission to change the model.

In Jeremy's case, the advice he got from our members was, "Get back to lean and mean." Cut down to where you were a year ago, get back to the clients that you enjoy working with, which provide you potentially the highest profit, and clear out all the other clutter. That means letting some clients and staff go. As hard as that is to do, if you're not sustainable going forward, then how are you going to help anybody?

Get your oxygen mask on first. Make sure it's working. Because if it fails for you, then everybody suffers. At some point, if you don't change the model, you're going to close down shop, and you won't survive it. Don't think it'll work out just by doing what you've been doing all along.

The Good Times: Stay the Course

When times are really good, we risk becoming complacent and confident—that's a toxic mix. We start taking risks that maybe in the long run we wouldn't have taken if the times weren't so good.

When we're complacent, we get careless, less discerning about capital expenditures or increases in overhead, just as Jeremy had been. Things were good a year before his crisis, so, without knowing his numbers or what metrics to look for, he started piling on: adding clients, staff, services. More and more.

As we learned in chapter 6, we must put our overall principles before strategies. We must use these conceptual filters even when times are good. You must measure where you are and what's happening at all times.

That's a big advantage of being a part of a mastermind group or other group where you share your concerns with like-minded owners or CEOs. These are folks with experience who know the good times don't last forever. They ask pointed questions such as, "Did you double-check this?" or "Are you sure about *why* you're doing this?"

When you report your business model and issues to a group, the feedback you get is valuable. Oftentimes, people who think things are going really well get a wake-up call. Without a "board of advisors" to support you, the time, frustration and actual monetary losses can be huge and destructive. Think back on a difficult time in your own life, when a business or an investment went bad— what would you have paid for advice that could have alleviated much or all of what you endured? And what about the other people around you—your family, spouse, and children? What price did they pay?

For example, one of our real estate group members has a solid business model in a certain geographic jurisdiction. When times were good, the member asked the group: "Should I apply this model to another municipality? How could I take this model and expand into other markets?"

The wisdom of our room agreed: be very, very careful. "Doing great" in one location in a roaring economy doesn't mean you're hitting the metrics to replicate the success in another—especially if there's a downturn. Just because you "think" you can or the economy's good, doesn't mean the venture will reflect well on your bottom line or on your personal freedom.

This is a common situation for dentists, when one will have a practice that is running well. He or she thinks, *If I just had another practice, then I could double everything. I'll double my money and work half the time!*

The opposite is what actually happens. Double the stress, half the net profits.

Be careful when veering out of your lane. During good times, it's easy for us to be caught up in what *could be* – new ventures, new markets, new clientele. While it sounds sexy, it's very difficult for most to achieve on the fly. Staying the course—and being accountable to others—keeps you from getting blindsided by the worst.

Planning for the Worst in Good Times

In 2019, our membership group saved a lot of people from making some questionable decisions at the height of good times.

That year, Freedom Founders had a major event themed "Prepare, Position, and Prosper." While the economy was raging hot – stock market up, real estate up, business up – we were helping our members take advantage of the good times *not* to grow more business but to prepare for the worst.

Over the course of two days, our members got honest about worst-case scenario situations. Even though the majority of this group was having their best year ever, they still took the time to share their worst fears, to second-guess their instincts to grow fast and throw away cash. *Should I really do that? Could I sustain my success even if business bottomed out?*

After the struggles of 2020, our members now look back at that event and agree: "I'm sure glad we did the work in advance!" And: "Although it wasn't easy, we were prepared and didn't have to panic!"

Going into the event, most were looking to stretch what they already had. Leaving the event, everyone was prepared to sustain the next downturn.

Thanks to the deep experience and wisdom of some of our members and advisors, the rest of our members were able to appreciate what can happen when good times come to an end. While keeping them cognizant of that fact, we had them look hard at their businesses and test their models, their run rate, profitability, and more against a loss of 10, 20, or even 30 percent revenue. *How would you have to shift things when the time comes?*

You have to make those shifts. A big part of shifting is expecting the shift to happen someday and having a Plan B ready to go. That way, you have the proper procedures in place to put out the fire before it burns the house down.

What You Learn in Down Times...

We have a big network of successful people who've been able to own their freedom. It's one thing to string together a few years where you feel free, but it's another to own your freedom for *decades*. It's remarkable how many of our members are starting to achieve that sort of next-level endurance, which also presents a great model to our younger members.

It's one thing to string together a few years where you feel free, but it's another to own your freedom for *decades*.

If I could sum up in one word the difference between our new members and the most experienced, I'd say: Confidence.

When we're younger, we don't know what we don't know. From about 2012 to early 2020, we had eight solid years of economic expansion. That's a pretty long period of time for the people who came into that era as young adults, maybe starting their career or business, if they hadn't been through a 2008 or something like it previously, then all they'd know is an upmarket. In other words, people who haven't experienced a down-market aren't even cognizant of the fact that there can be tougher times.

Confidence builds with time. The other way to gain a certain level of confidence is by being with other people who have the wisdom and the track record. If you're willing to listen to them, take their wisdom in stride, and understand that good times will come to an end at some point, then at least you've got some mental preparation.

That said, you'll have to go through a major correction as an adult, see how that feels, and get through it one way or the other before you develop true confidence in your ability to sustain through difficult or bad times.

Getting through bad times at least once gives you a certain level of confidence that you could do it again. It makes you more aware of what you need to know going forward without becoming complacent.

And once you're on the other side of it, you'll question the risks of expanding too soon or too fast.

Prioritize Your Legacy

How is legacy an extension of owning your freedom?

When things are going well – the business, the personal finances, the investments, and everything else – we can get caught up in wanting to push harder.

We see opportunity. *I can do more. I can gain more. I can stockpile more. Grow my material wealth. Make my business better.*

Oftentimes, our lifestyle expands. We think, "I'm doing well, so I'm justified in moving to the bigger house in the better neighborhood and getting the better cars and the vacation home." After working hard, sacrificing for years, and putting school first, with the good times at hand, you're justified in expanding your lifestyle, right?

Then the tide turns.

A personal or external crisis hits and suddenly you don't need the vacation house or the better car. You realize—what if I'd focused on *freedom* instead of stockpiling more?

That's where legacy comes in. When times are good, you don't just have the opportunity to push harder for more. You have the opportunity to finally build your legacy.

Our Freedom Founders membership group rallied after the Spring 2020 lockdown. By the end of 2020, most of them had met (and had exceeded) their yearly financial goals.

Some might see success as an opportunity to change lifestyle, spending more lavishly. Instead, our members took survival as a marker that they're neither impenetrable nor infallible.

The consensus was: *we dodged a bullet*. It's made each member think about legacy: *What's important today? What do I really want?*

The trick is to ask "What do I really want?" when times are good. Then make it happen—don't put it off.

Build Your Legacy Today

A lot of people think legacy is something you *leave*. The typical idea is material wealth, given when you pass, which you prepare through estate planning. But that's only one part of legacy.

The other part is the fact that we're actually living our legacy today, every day. What wisdom and support can you pass on while you're still here? This type of legacy is one you can do on a smaller basis. If you have kids or grandkids, mentors or big brothers – whatever you're doing, whoever you're interacting with – is there somebody whom you can impart some wisdom to in the right way? On a regular basis?

> How are you going to pass on what you've learned? You can't wait until the end to pass on that type of legacy. You must be thinking about it today.

I believe legacy serves as the answer to: *How are you going to pass on what you've learned?* You can't wait until the end to pass on that type of legacy. You must be thinking about it today.

How to build your legacy today:

1. Know what you want (Freedom).
2. Discover your purpose.
3. Use your purpose to achieve your freedom.

Know What You Want (Freedom)

What do I want now? If I want to own my freedom, then why? What are my personal reasons? What's the ultimate legacy of my freedom and ownership?

Freedom gives you a lot of opportunities to build your legacy on a daily basis. It's how you achieve what you want to leave at the end of life.

Discover Your Purpose

What's my real purpose? Why do I want it? Who do I need to become? Who do I need to know? How do I need to improve my self to own more freedom?

To get clarity on what you want and why you want it, you may have to change. Reflect, meet new people, have deeper conversations, seek improvement—these actions will spark the change that helps you discover your purpose.

It takes courage to look inside and say, "I am who I am today, and this is what I'm made for."

It's not about beating yourself up. It's not about being self-destructive. It's just saying "I'm successful to the point I am at today, wherever that is. But, gee, there's so much more to me."

Use Your Purpose to Achieve Your Freedom

Don't wait! America is still a land of opportunity where you get to own your own self-education, how you think, your selected associations and wealth strategies, and more. You have a choice. You can "decide" to engage your own opportunities through the principles laid out in this book, or you can abdicate your future and freedom to others.

Achieving and maintaining freedom means one needs to think, prepare, and organize for the life one wants to live in the near future, not just the life being lived now.

Peace of Mind

The best part of owning your freedom and living a legacy every day? Peace of mind.

Bronnie Ware is an Australian palliative care nurse who wrote the best-selling book, *The Top Five Regrets of the Dying*. She interviewed a number of her patients in hospice care, many of whom were business owners. Over the course of a few weeks of conversation during their end-of-life care, she was able to ask some deep questions. She compiled the answers and conversations in her book, which captures the regrets shared by those who've gone before us.

What she found was the top five regrets had nothing to do with a bigger business, more money or wealth, or bigger investments. They were all about time, relationships, and not living for other people's agendas.

When you own your freedom, you have peace of mind to focus on building a legacy for those you leave behind.

For me, I'm a natural-born driver. I get up in the morning with a revved engine, ready to go. But rather than spend my time doing anything, I have to ask myself, *why do I do what I do?*

I'm blessed. I don't do what I do because I need the money. I also don't need to go build something bigger because I need a monument to myself. I might've done that earlier in life because society admires those who prove themselves in a big way. But you can't take it with you.

That's why owning your freedom is *enough*. Being Free for Life™ is *enough*.

It gives us peace of mind. It allows me to turn my "drive to build more" into the "drive to build legacy."

"Enough" is enough when you can let go of the chase for more and move on to what's most important to you.

"Enough" is enough when you can let go of the chase for more, and move on to what's most important to you.

A final word on Bronnie Ware: Many of the business owners she interviewed never found their peace of mind. Until the end they were always driving, always worried, chasing money to the grave. All this worry should teach us something.

In 2020 during Covid-19, I saw plenty of worry in our membership groups as well. It was a difficult time across the board. On our Zoom calls, I saw faces full of concern and stress. Concern not just for themselves but for their staff and clients. They worried about the other people who were relying on them. They carried the torch to get through this thing one way or the other, giving it their all so that they could have a business and a place to go to work on the other side.

Then, as we marched on to the other side of this with great care and concern, I saw a new perspective emerge. Our members had a new expression on their faces. Looking back, they spoke of how they rediscovered what really mattered. Looking forward, they shared a newfound sense of their priorities: *more quality time, more purpose, more legacy, more memories.* Nobody was talking about overextending to chase the next opportunity. Everyone just wanted more freedom.

With that perspective came waves of relief. In later calls, I saw a qualitative reduction of stress. No longer did they hold onto some imaginary pinnacle of wealth. Peace of mind prevailed.

What's Most Important

Dr. Hiru Mathur, a periodontist, and her husband Sumit have two boys, ages 18 and 25. Sumit runs a software business while Hiru leads the dental practice. I talked to them both on the phone as I was writing this chapter.

As we were talking about their Freedom Number and blueprint, Hiru reiterated how the pandemic gave them the opportunity to spend a lot more time with her boys, who were home from school where they otherwise wouldn't have been.

In spending time together, Hiru got a glimpse of what life could be like if she wasn't working full time at her practice.

After discussing her blueprint, Hiru realized she's in the position to hire two part-time associates in her practice. She'll have to give up some revenue to buy back her time, but it's worth it. Rather than selling her practice, she's retooling her model so that it's not all about her. One of the associates is experienced and can help with the workload, while the other is a younger doctor who's learning from the two mentors. This setup allows Hiru to focus on the clients and procedures she prefers.

She expected a reduction in her active income because of the new hires but has been pleasantly surprised to find her income actually has gone up. On top of that, she's also learned how to build wealth outside of the practice. As a Freedom Founders member, she's seen success already in building passive income through real estate.

She said recently, "I can now take my foot off the pedal and start to own my freedom. I'm going to own my freedom *now*. Not in 10 years. Not in 15 years. I'm going to own it now. And that means I get the opportunity to make some decisions differently today than I would have a year ago."

Where does she see herself going? What sort of freedom is she experiencing and picturing?

Like a lot of people who have worked a full career and are close to owning their freedom, she had reached the point where much of the day-to-day started to become a drag. *I've got to show up. I've tasks to do. I've got to make the money.*

By following the principles of owning your freedom, she's arrived in a place where the dental practice that used to be a hassle has become enjoyable anew.

And because of the pandemic, she's grown into a much better leader. Her husband Sumit said, "It used to be that she was very much an appeaser who didn't like conflict, and who therefore abdicated some of the leadership role. Well, Covid-19 required business owners to step up in many ways that were new. Now she's owning her leadership role. And it feels good because she's earned a higher-level respect from her employees. She's got a staff she enjoys. They enjoy her." They're in it together, which is a great time to bring on another doctor—when you're running things well, not when things are a mess.

The important point is that Hiru is doing it *now*.

In return for giving up some of the revenue and patient load, she's getting the time she wants, so she can focus on the things in life that are most important to her.

Meanwhile, she's still working and leading. Like many of us, she's not ready to cut the cord completely. She's not selling the practice. She remains a leader who impacts her patients and staff. And she's buying herself more time with her family.

> Visit www.OwnYourFreedomBook.com/Resources for the free training in which Hiru and I discuss the specific strategies and steps she took to achieve freedom by investing passively in real estate without the hassles of fixing toilets or having to deal with tenants.

THE JOURNEY TO OWN YOUR FREEDOM:

DR. NATHAN HO

"*If anyone can do it, I can too.*"

That's Dr. Nathan Ho's life motto. And that's the attitude needed to integrate the five principles to own your freedom.

At age twelve, Nathan immigrated with his family to the US from Vietnam. He didn't have much money and couldn't speak much English, but he did have ambition, hope, and a solid work ethic. "I didn't have much guidance as far as what to do when I grew up because we didn't have any college graduates in our family," he recalled in an interview with me for this book. But when he found out his cousin intended to pursue dentistry, he thought, *"If anyone can do it, I can too."*

Upon graduating dental school, Nathan noted how "most of my classmates were looking for a job, but I was looking for a dental practice to buy, not because I had the knowledge, but because I thought that *if other people could do it, I could as well.* And a few months later, I bought a small dental practice with a classmate. Three months later, we started the new practice in the city."

So right off the bat, Dr. Ho utilized *Principle #2: The Power of Association.* He chose to go into business with a partner, not alone. When they hit the usual struggles in the first two years, his business partner talked about closing up shop. But Dr. Ho knew that once they improved their marketing skills, the business could pick up, and they would succeed. "And sure enough," he told me, "after we figured out the marketing strategy, our business went vertical, and we were able to pay off all our debts. I became debt-free in my early thirties."

"I became debt-free in my early thirties."

Dr. Ho taught himself how to market his dental practices and utilized *Principle #5: Invest in Your Transferable Skill Sets.* To do this, he observed how other dental practices marketed themselves and adopted their methods, such as hosting events.

This strategy also utilized *Principle #4: Principles before Strategies, Strategies before Tactics.* Dr. Ho knew he wanted to advertise, but he wasn't sure of the strategy or tactic. So he copied what worked for his competition, and it worked for him too. He paid attention. He observed. And then he took action.

By this point, Dr. Ho had a steady cash flow. All the while, he was thinking about *Principle #1: Your Freedom Number*—what was his? How much money would be enough to sustain the lifestyle he wanted?

He had already taught himself marketing, had a steady business partner, and possessed years of training in a technical skill. "I love what I do in dentistry," he said. "I love transforming smiles and improving lives. But I don't want to tie myself to that eight hours a day, five days a week." Plus, he had heard that most dentists eventually suffered from neck and back pain, and he wanted to avoid getting to that point.

So with the mindset of, *"If anyone can do it, I can too,"* why not get into the technology side of the business and pursue other business opportunities? Expanding his already open mindset, Dr. Ho "realized that there are so many opportunities for so many people to do well, to build a future for themselves and their families." This mindset put his Freedom Number in reach.

One of those opportunities was EnvisionStars. Dr. Ho had learned the importance of positive reviews for his dental practice. Greater client engagement meant better business. So with two other co-founders, Dr. Ho created EnvisionStars, a customer engagement platform to help small businesses get more referrals, positive reviews, and more consistent engagement with their existing and new customers. Dr. Ho was helping other business owners grow their businesses and own their freedom, too.

Pursuing other opportunities meant shifting further from the dentist mindset to the CEO mindset. That required utilizing skills he wasn't trained in, like leadership and management. So he revisited *Principle #5: Invest in Your Transferable Skill Sets.* With generalized skills such as leadership and management, he learned by doing, and he steadily improved over time.

"Over time I learned about leadership, how to lead a team, and how to be a leader in my business. I learned how to manage a team and how to create a system so the business can run by itself without us having to come up with new strategies and train people. And I learned how to develop and scale my business."

He also learned leadership by seeking out mentors. Delving back into *Principle #2: The Power of Association*, his mentors taught Dr. Ho what he needed for his new skill sets in leadership and management. He knew it could take someone "years, or a lifetime, to achieve success. But if you work with a mentor, then that person can actually help you accelerate your success in a year or two."

Learning from mentors and peers prevents you from making costly mistakes and saves you time. Dr. Ho leveraged other people's success and skills to help shorten his learning curve. "The main reason I was able to do all this was thanks to relationships. I can't even put a value to it."

And in making the shift from practitioner to CEO, he was no longer dependent upon trading time for dollars. He could make money by making decisions.

In making the shift from practitioner to CEO, he was no longer dependent upon trading time for dollars. He could make money by making decisions.

Dr. Ho's experience is a prime example of living the principles of Own Your Freedom. The five core priciples taught are not necessarily meant to be completed in order, but in parallel. The principles as a whole are intended to be repeated as you continue through your freedom journey.

When circumstances are out of your control—like during the pandemic—you *can* control the development of your own skills and knowledge. So for Dr. Ho, it was under his control during the COVID-19 pandemic to learn how to become a better public speaker.

"I'm currently spending some time and money to invest in public speaking so I can influence and help share my stories and business strategies and experience to help other entrepreneurs, or to inspire other people out there to be more successful and to think for themselves."

And while investing in your personal development may not always seem business-related, Dr. Ho found that it all connects. "When I'm not working in the business, I work on myself. For example, during COVID, a lot of people gained weight because they ate more. But for me, I said, 'This is the best time to exercise, I have more time than ever!' And I got into the best shape of my life. I also had more time to spend with my kids, and more time to read. During that time, I invested in myself, so when I came back, I came back stronger, with a better skill set, and more energy to make more money."

To mitigate the income drop caused by the pandemic shutdown, Dr. Ho continued to focus on what he could control. He learned more about *Principle #3: Wealth Is What You Own, Not What You Do*, and how to manage risk in that field. He also started up a PPE supply business in just three days!

The dental field, short on masks during the COVID-19 pandemic, had a moment of panic. But Dr. Ho believes "whenever you see problems, there are opportunities, because if you can provide solutions to those problems, then you can build a business to serve the markets where the problems exist."

So he jumped in with both feet. "I called some manufacturers, did my due diligence, and launched a dental supply business within about three days."

He told me it was "a win-win because we were able to help our colleagues in getting the supplies they needed to see patients, and we made a profit in doing that. So there are opportunities everywhere. We just have to look for them. But the key thing is to take action because timing is very important. Had I waited and sat on it for three months, then the outcome would have been different."

Had Dr. Ho not taken action on his business idea, someone else would have filled the void and reaped the profit. But he didn't let the moment pass him by. He owned the moment.

Because Dr. Ho owns his freedom.

He used to take one day off per week, but because of his success he was able to reduce his active labor by a second day because of his success. Instead of having his nose to the grindstone through the workweek, Dr. Ho can put his feet up on Wednesdays and Thursdays. He chose days off that work for him.

Dr. Ho knows that "opportunities will come that you didn't plan for." So being mentally prepared for those opportunities is key. His "if anyone can do it, I can too" attitude *applied to the five principles* has given him both sustainability and freedom. He enjoys multiple streams of income from EnvisionStars, his dental practices, his technology, and medical supply businesses, and soon, real estate.

"I think owning your own freedom is very important. That's the only way to have more options in life, so you can have more time with your family, work on projects that interest you, and do what you want."

THE JOURNEY
TO OWN YOUR
FREEDOM:

DR. TOM
JOVICICH

'm privileged to know Tom Jovicich, who owns his freedom. Dr. Tom is a dentist and business owner, who over the past few years has shifted to investor. Today he owns a type of real estate different from the single-family homes I've mentioned thus far in the book: a storage center of mobile pod-like units.

The path to ownership wasn't easy—two divorces, burnout, surgeries, and too much time spent trading hours for dollars. Mid-career, having reached a low-point, Tom knew he had to find better.

"A lot of times it's pain that pushes us to do one of two things: either we hunker down, go inside, and don't do anything, or we're propelled forward."

For many years, Tom had lacked the cash to invest in the real estate market locally in southern California. "I never thought I had enough money to get into real estate—homes, apartments, or other properties."

Tom's situation changed in 2016 when he was offered cash for his house—an amount that exceeded his expectations. "Because of my history of two divorces, at the time I was living basically paycheck to paycheck—there wasn't a huge cache of money that you would think someone in his early fifties would have."

What to do with the sudden windfall? "One of my good friends at the time was very successful. But his success all came from financial instruments. And so, he introduced me to his wealth management strategist.

"I remember the day I put the money in the market: May 15, 2016. It was the worst day for the market. I went instantly from seven figures down to six figures."

If he'd been a younger man, Tom might have let the money ride for a few decades and accumulated "enough to retire." "But for a fifty-something-year-old," he said, "that model wasn't going to work." Tom realized the hard way he had put tactics before strategy—doing the opposite of *Principle #4: Principles before Strategies, Strategies before Tactics.*

So he rethought his approach. Seeking principles and strategies, he joined Freedom Founders.

Tom always had on his mind *Principle #3: Wealth is What You Own, Not What You Do.* "Part of what I learned in Freedom Founders is to make your money work for you. Always keep it working, dividing it up, to provide cash flow. I also learned that the stock market and financial assets just don't always work. Like many of us, I was basically brainwashed to believe the only way to accumulate wealth for people like us is with a financial manager. Because we own our business and work mostly honing our craft, I'm not going to sit there and watch the stock market daily, doing my due diligence on what Apple is producing that's going to affect their bottom line or what Texas Instruments is going to do. Instead, I should pay someone to do that for me. So if someone says, 'Tom, give me your million dollars, I'll invest it for you, we'll meet three times a year. I'll send you a nice dozen golf balls and maybe we'll play tennis, maybe go to a Dodger game,' I say, 'Wow, that's great. Thank you. You're going to be my steward.' But there's so much blind faith that you have to pay attention to—the keyword being 'blind.'

So the hard lesson to learn was I had to lose money to realize I'm not at the right age class for this type of investment opportunity. I'm in the wrong place. And I'm also someone who likes to be a little bit more hands-on.

> ## I had to lose money to realize I'm not at the right age class for this type of investment opportunity. I'm in the wrong place.

Many of us get to our late 40s, 50s, and 60s and experience the real, dreaded feeling of *no control*—and we want control in our lives, do we not? We're built for control. But in this financial world, we have no control. And that dreaded feeling sets in when you realize your savings are tied up in Wall Street assets that provide you no cash flow or flexibility."

His journey to owning a storage facility started with *Principle #2: The Power of Association*, by meeting someone in our group Freedom Founders. Through that meeting, Tom was connected to two mentors who own several extremely successful storage facilities in the Bay Area, and who showed Tom what it would take to buy a facility of his own.

As a business owner and investor, Tom leaned on his non-specialized skills, which is *Principle #5: Invest in Your Transferable Skill Sets.* For Tom, his primary skill set was negotiation.

As Tom said: "Negotiation—that is just life from the get-go. How many people don't ever practice the good art of negotiation? It's as simple as understanding the value you bring and how you can orchestrate a win-win proposition by learning how to move the pieces around so that the value becomes equalized based on what someone else wants. Price matters less once everyone's comfortable with value. And no one teaches you that."

Being new to the investing and storage business, Tom again relied on the power of association. "Whenever you run into an uncertain situation, you don't just figure it out on your own. You're going to go back out to the people who you surround yourself with on purpose and say, 'Hey, I'm faced with this—could be a challenge, could be an opportunity. But give me some feedback.' I just need quick feedback and someone to give me a little more clarity about how I'm looking at things. And oftentimes, that instantaneous clarity gives us a direction to go with. Problem solved. Or at least I'm in the right direction to eventually solving it."

For example, when Tom had a minor personnel crisis at the storage facility, he called up all his mentors, and within 24 hours, had new personnel on-site.

Today, Tom knows his Freedom Number, which is *Principle #1.* "Freedom for me is $20,000 a month after all expenses. If I can do that, I can live quite well. Ownership got me there. Doing my due diligence, finding the storage property, and supporting its management hasn't been easy. But I learned a lot along the way. Now we're expanding. While I wasn't ready to expand in 2020, in 2021, we're adding another 5,000 square feet of rentable units."

So, what's going to fulfill Tom in the years ahead? What will he do now that he owns his freedom?

Tom is still *Dr. Jovicich*, owner of his successful dental practice. The next five years will likely see him transition from practice ownership to focusing on his legacy.

"My hope is I'm able to pass on the facilities to each of my kids. A legacy by ensuring their future is under control. And now that our churches are opening up after the pandemic, I'm back to doing activities with my kids, being able to take care of the homeless. We're interacting with people and helping those who are less fortunate than us.

"Then on the personal side of life, I'll be happy to work three days a week, three weeks a month. I also want to be gone one week a month somewhere in the world."

What would Tom say to someone starting out on the journey to own their freedom? I'll let him have the last word:

> *"I would say you need to be able to think outside the box. Because the path you're on currently is in a box. Your family, your church, your life, your business—these are all within a certain box. And if you're so ingrained in working within that box, you get very comfortable, which also means you get blindsided by disruption.*

If you're so ingrained in working within that box, you get very comfortable, which also means you get blindsided by disruption.

Back when I was 20 years old, I was going to be married with kids, have a house in California, a house in Telluride, and be able to go anywhere I wanted. God gave me a dose of reality on that one. Twice.

When we plan, God laughs. None of my plans have ever worked out. But having faith and being willing to be vulnerable always does. They've gotten me to where God wants me to be right now.

So if you want freedom in your life, you have to have an open heart and an open mind. If you can't do those things, you'll never truly have freedom—you'll just be that hamster in the wheel, logging miles. How sad for people who don't get that, and then look back on their life when they're towards the end and have all those regrets, wondering, "Why didn't I take some chances? Why didn't I change the way I was doing things?"

If you're thinking outside the box, opportunities present themselves. Then you just have to be willing to pivot. Be willing to be vulnerable. Do it even with zero knowledge. As long as you have mentors, a willingness to learn, and a goal, you can seize the opportunity.

It doesn't always work the first time. But if you don't try anything, then no change or transformation will ever happen. You've got to put yourself out there to be vulnerable.

Think outside the box and be willing to be vulnerable—that's where your success comes from. Every time."

ABOUT THE AUTHOR: DR. DAVID PHELPS

WHO IS DR. DAVID PHELPS?
AND WHY SHOULD YOU LISTEN TO
HIM ABOUT YOUR FREEDOM?

A PRACTICE OWNER TURNED
CEO AND LEADER

David owned and managed a private practice dental office for over twenty-one years before his daughter's health crisis served as a dramatic wakeup call in his life. David's "Plan B" (a portfolio of cash-flow producing real estate assets) gave him the Freedom to sell his practice mid-career and focus 100 percent on what matters most to him.

As a protege of Dan Kennedy, David is a renegade – he does not follow the majority but lives life and does business on his own terms and is not dictated to by others.

AMERICA'S #1 AUTHORITY ON CREATING
FREEDOM IN LIFE AND BUSINESS

David is the author of six published business, finance, and success books. As a nationally-recognized keynote speaker, David brings dynamic energy and unique insights into how to create financial freedom through passive income, how to build a real business that doesn't take over your life, anti-traditional real estate investing, private lending, wealth-building legacy, and how to take responsibility and "own" your life.

A LEADER BORN THROUGH CRISIS

Sitting with his daughter in the hospital room after her battle with leukemia and a life-saving liver transplant, Dr. David Phelps realized what matters most. It was not his career as a dentist that had consumed his daily life for over twenty-one years. He needed to be present for his daughter, Jenna.

He decided he would no longer practice dentistry. Instead, he was able to pivot to his Plan B.

He drew inspiration from his years of investing avidly in real estate that began in dental school with a joint-venture investment with his father. By leveraging the lessons and capital he had acquired, David built an investment portfolio that could generate enough passive income to leave his dental practice and be the father his daughter needed.

AN ESCAPEE OF THE DOLLARS-FOR-HOURS TRAP

David's radical new life intrigued his peers, who asked him how they too could command control of their wealth and time. By bringing together his two worlds—high-income medical professionals and real estate professionals—David created a powerful network of like-minded professionals who could support each other on their own paths to financial and personal freedom.

He called this group Freedom Founders, and as its leader he found his purpose: helping his colleagues break the chains of bondage to their practices and financial fears and create freedom in their lives.

With his own life as proof, David challenges the traditional model of wealth building, which preaches abdicating control over one's money to advisors and entrusting all of one's investing capital to Wall Street.

David has witnessed too many high-income professionals blindly trust the traditional path only to have their hard-earned wealth wiped out by the volatility of the public market. Through Freedom Founders, David exhorts his members to take back control of their investing capital from their practices and 401(k) plans, put it to work in more stable, capital producing assets like real estate, and to always stay focused on their own freedom.

FREE FOR LIFE™

Freedom Founders Mastermind Group began as a meeting of sixteen people over a decade ago and has grown into a community of over one hundred members and Trusted Advisors, where David's insights into the financial markets, alternative investing, and achieving success and fulfillment in life attract freedom-seeking members from across the country.

Speaking from his own experience, (David is the "product of the product"), David strives to instill in his members the courage to lead lives unhindered by the expectations of others and driven by purpose. Following in his footsteps, Freedom Founders members attain the tools to become Free for Life™: they can live entirely on the passive income from their real estate investments.

A RECOGNIZED LEADER IN DENTISTRY AND REAL ESTATE

David has been featured in Advantage ForbesBooks, The Profitable Dentist, Dental Success Today, The Progressive Orthodontist, MarketWatch,

Business Insider, Markets Insider, Value Investing News, Morningstar, Yahoo! Finance, and Entrepreneur magazine, among others. He has been awarded the GKIC Marketer of the Year (2011) award.

He regularly keynotes and presents at live events, and has co-hosted multiple virtual and webinar conferences. He is frequently asked to guest present at niche industry mastermind meetings.

David regularly collaborates with countless industry leaders including Dr. Dustin Burleson, Dr. David Maloley, Dr. Michael Abernathy, Dan Sullivan, Steven J Anderson, Scott Manning, Alastair Macdonald, Dr. Scott Leune, Jason Medley, Shaun McCloskey, Eddie Speed, Daniel Marcos, Christopher Ryan, Dr. John Meis, Dr. Christopher Phelps, and countless others.

At his own events, he has shared the stage with Garrett Gunderson, Chuck Blakeman, Adam Witty, Dr. Dustin Burleson, Dr. David Moffet, Dr. David Maloley, Mike Michalowicz, Tony Rubleski, Jim Palmer, Thomas Blackwell, and many others.

AN EXPERT IN THE WORLD OF REAL ESTATE

David's expertise in the world of real estate includes everything from multi-family apartments, self-storage, commercial properties, mobile home parks, retail properties, single-family rentals, structured notes, private debt, managed funds, and more. He has successfully weathered multiple market corrections – notably using the 2006-2008 downturn to successfully more than double his net worth.

He is regularly consulted in the creation, structure, and economics of large multi-investor syndications, funds, and private investments secured by real estate assets.

ABOUT THE CO-AUTHOR: DAN S. KENNEDY

WHO IS DAN KENNEDY?
AND WHY SHOULD YOU LISTEN TO HIM
ABOUT YOUR MONEY?

FROM THE WORLD OF PROFESSIONAL PRACTICE & DOLLARS-FOR-HOURS

Nearly his entire working life, Dan Kennedy has operated a three-part professional practice as a marketing consultant, advertising copywriter, and public speaker. "I fully understand," Kennedy says, "how difficult it is for those of us conditioned in this way to then break the Work-Money Link."

CELEBRATED AUTHOR

Dan Kennedy is the author of over 30 published business and success books. He has somewhat miraculously *never* been absent from bookstore shelves from 1981-Present. His NO BS series is one of the most popular business book series, spanning 2004 to Present, and placing on Amazon, Wall Street Journal and other Bestseller Lists as well as on INC. Magazine's 100 Best Business Books List. His most recent book is: *ALMOST ALCHEMY: Make Any Business of Any Size Produce More with Fewer and Less* by ForbesBooks

CONSULTANT & DIRECT RESPONSE ADVERTISING COPYWRITER

Dan has been directly, integrally involved with legacy and newly built brands you're familiar with, like Weight Watchers and Proactiv, but also hundreds of entrepreneurs' enterprises, built from scratch to multi-million dollar and even billion-dollar values. As a sought-after Marketing Strategy Consultant, his recent and current fees begin at $3,300 per hour or $18,800 per day for in-person or teleconsulting, and, per project, integrating copywriting for every offline and online media, upwards from $100,000. His current and ongoing clients include niche-industry consulting/coaching firms working with thousands of solo and small law practices, dentists, and other professional practice owners; HealthSource, the largest franchisor in chiropractic; and High Point University. For about a decade, Dan was extremely active in developing, writing for, and producing TV infomercials, and he has scripted and put words in the mouths of nearly 100 different celebrity spokespersons.

POPULAR SPEAKER

Kennedy has delivered over 3000 compensated engagements in the U.S. and abroad, including a nine-year stint on the #1 public seminar tour of all time, visiting 20-27 cities a year, held mostly in NBA stadiums, with audiences of 15,000 to 25,000.

He has appeared repeatedly with four former U.S. Presidents including Ronald Reagan and other world leaders, Hollywood celebrities, sports champions, and the legendary business speakers Zig Ziglar,

Brian Tracy, Jim Rohn, and Tom Hopkins, as well as Donald Trump (pre-presidency) and the founders of companies like Mrs. Fields Cookies and 1-800-Flowers.

At his own conferences and events, he appeared with celebrity entrepreneurs John Rich, Gene Simmons (KISS), Joan Rivers, George Foreman, Kathy Ireland, and Ivanka Trump.

SERIAL ENTREPRENEUR

On the back of his speaking, Dan built one of the largest "information marketing," publishing, conferences, membership, and coaching companies, with his NO BS MARKETING LETTER as its centerpiece. Although still involved, he masterminded the sale of the company three times, once to Private Equity; it now resides at ADVANTAGE, with Advantage and ForbesBooks. As a Serial Entrepreneur, he has also started, built, bought, and sold other businesses, and derived royalties from the launch or growth of over 100 different companies via his consulting.

EXPERIENCED & SUCCESSFUL
INDEPENDENT INVESTOR

Kennedy has been involved in start-ups as an investor, notably including the extremely successful small business/marketing software company Infusionsoft/Kaep. His diversified investment portfolio includes apartment buildings and commercial properties, equities, structured notes, private debt, managed funds, and hobby investments in collector cars, and rare and first edition books, including books by Napoleon Hill, Dale Carnegie, David Ogilvy, and P.T. Barnum.

In 30-plus years' investing, he has never had a negative year, and in the past 10 years has averaged year over year gains of 20-plus percent.

"FRIEND" OF DENTISTRY

Almost 10,000 dentists attended Dan Kennedy's SuccessTrak Seminars, from 1981-1987, and he has continued to have many dentists as Members of the NO BS INNER CIRCLE to this day. He has also been, at different times, in some cases for many years, the "consultant to the consultants," advising leaders of the field including Dr. Tom Orent, Dr. Dustin Burleson, Linda Miles, Jay Geier and The Scheduling Institute, Dr. David Phelps and Freedom Founders, and others. It is nearly impossible to attend a coaching group or mastermind meeting in the profession without hearing Dan Kennedy referenced!

RESOURCES

Whenever you're ready, here are additional ways I can help fast-track your journey to Own Your Freedom:

1. Hear more from me through books, podcast, and blogs.

- *From High Income To High Net Worth: Alternative Investment Strategies to Stop Trading Time for Dollars and Start Creating True Freedom* by Dr. David Phelps, www.HighIncomeBook.com

- *What's Your Next?: The Blueprint For Creating Your Freedom Lifestyle* by Dr. David Phelps, www.FindYourNext.com

- *The Apprentice Model: A Young Leader's Guide to an Anti-Traditional Life* by Dr. David Phelps, www.ApprenticeModelBook.com

- *The Dentist Freedom Blueprint* podcast, www.DentistFreedomBlueprint.com

- For quick-hitting videos and articles for those looking to jump-start their freedom journey, visit www.FreedomFounders.com/Blog

2. Watch my online training for more of the Five Principles found within *Own Your Freedom*.

You've read the book but are you ready to fully develop the Five Core Principles of Owning Your Freedom? I've created a special training that's free of cost and will supercharge your journey to freedom: www.OwnYourFreedomBook.com/Resources

3. Schedule a call with me.

If you'd like to replace your active income with passive investment income within two to three years, and you have at least $1 million in available capital (which can include residential, practice, and business equity), then go to the following link to schedule a call with my team. If it looks like there is a mutual fit, you'll have an opportunity to schedule a call with me directly: www.FreedomFounders.com/Schedule

4. Get your free Retirement Scorecard.

Benchmark your retirement and wealth-building against hundreds of other practice professionals and business owners. Get personalized feedback on your biggest opportunities and leverage points. Go to www.FreedomFounders.com/Scorecard to take the three-minute assessment and get your scorecard.

5. Receive my monthly newsletter: Path to Freedom.

Get "inside access" to the strategies used by hundreds of dentists, doctors, and practice professionals to create a combined millions of dollars of passive income. This publication is packed with strategies, principles, and techniques. It's an easy 30-minute read that will expand your mind and unlock wealth-building potential to catapult you from high income to high net worth. Mailed every month, it's a power-packed resource: www.PathToFreedomNewsletter.com

6. Apply to visit the Freedom Founders Community.

If you'd like to join dozens of dentists, doctors, and practice professionals on the fast track to freedom (three to five years or less), visit www.FreedomFounders.com/Step-1 to apply for a guest seat.

7. Work with me directly.

If you'd like to work directly with me and a small group of my closest investment colleagues, with direct access to the dealmakers and asset classes that I invest in, message me at admin@FreedomFounders.com and put "Fast Access" in the subject line. Or call (972) 203-6960 (ext. 160) and leave a brief message. Let us know you're interested in the Fast Access program—we'll set up a time with you to talk, find out about your goals, and see if there's a fit.